D1274239

THE
Community
Builders

ENVIRONMENTAL DESIGN AND DEVELOPMENT SERIES

❊ ❊ ❊

A CONTRIBUTION FROM THE COLLEGE OF ENVIRONMENTAL DESIGN
UNIVERSITY OF CALIFORNIA, BERKELEY

THE
Community
Builders

EDWARD P. EICHLER

and

MARSHALL KAPLAN

UNIVERSITY OF CALIFORNIA PRESS
BERKELEY, LOS ANGELES, LONDON

UNIVERSITY OF CALIFORNIA PRESS
Berkeley and Los Angeles, California

UNIVERSITY OF CALIFORNIA PRESS, Ltd.
London, England

Copyright © 1967, by The Regents of the University of California

THIRD PRINTING, 1974

DESIGNED BY IRVING PERKINS

Standard Book Number 520-00380-2

Library of Congress Catalog Card Number: 67-13601

Printed in the United States of America

To the three people who made us their protegés,
for good or for bad:

CHARLES ABRAMS   JOSEPH L. EICHLER
and
THE LATE CATHERINE BAUER WURSTER

Preface

ON JULY 1, 1963, The Center for Planning and Development Research at the Berkeley campus of the University of California submitted "A Proposal for a Demonstration Program in Urban Development" to the Ford Foundation, requesting $200,000 to be spent over an 18-month period. The Foundation approved this project, which came to be known as the "Community Development Project," and which I agreed to direct, as of February 1, 1964.

This book is, in part, the story of that project; perhaps the best way to begin is with a brief description of the backgrounds of the authors and of the Project.

The Authors

Between 1951 and 1964, I helped manage a family-controlled homebuilding company in California—Eichler homes, Inc. During that time I traveled a good deal within and without the United States, viewing the operations of many builders and discussing with them ways to improve the industry both in its own structure and in its contribution to public policy. Consistently active in liberal politics, I also testified for the Americans for Democratic Action in 1961 on housing legislation then pending in Congress. In the fall of that year I was appointed Chairman of the (California) Governor's Advisory Commission on Housing Problems.[1]

---

[1] After completion of this study, I returned to Eichler Homes. Recently, I assumed the role of vice president for Reston, Virginia. Marshall Kaplan is a principal in the economic analysis and planning firm of Marshall Kaplan, Gans, and Kahn, San Francisco.

Marshall Kaplan, who holds M.A. degrees in political science and in city planning, has worked in the planning department of the cities of Louisville, Kentucky, and San Diego, California, and, like myself, has been active in liberal politics. We met when he became the Report Coordinator of the Governor's Housing Commission.

The Governor's Advisory Commission on Housing

The Commission contracted for studies covering a variety of issues such as population trends, land-use controls, the mortgage market in California, and changes in land prices. Those of us who determined the Commission's perspective felt that the Report should be concerned with the following issues:

1. That public policy had over-emphasized redevelopment and should now concern itself with growth at metropolitan fringes—an issue especially important to a rapidly growing state such as California.
2. That the absence of inexpensive housing in new fringe areas was forcing low and moderate-income families to commute from older parts of the city to jobs in the suburbs. This was not only inequitable financially, but also exacerbated forces already making central cities the home of the poor and non-white, and the suburbs those of middle- and upper-income whites.
3. That this cleavage was caused chiefly by the high, and rising, cost of new housing—especially soaring land prices —and by the absence of a large stock of older housing to accommodate rapid growth; that the so-called process of filtering (whereby lower-income families presumably get access to better used housing) did not, and could not, work.
4. Finally, that the most urgent, though by no means the only, objective of the State's housing programs should be to devise means to give low- and moderate-income families access to new housing in outlying areas.

With these issues in mind, some of the consultants, the staff, and various commission members felt that the question of "new towns" was relevant. If Western European nations, with relative stable populations, could undertake a new-towns program which entailed moving populations from one part of a country to another, why could not California more easily do the same? Since both industry and housing were involved, it was conceivable that such a program could considerably minimize California's housing problems. This thinking produced two proposed programs.

Under the first, the State itself would purchase large blocks of land (or charter a public corporation to do so), install public facilities, and then sell the land to private developers for housing, commerce, and industry. The plan required that a certain portion of the land be sold only to builders (or to public or non-profit agencies) who would provide low-cost housing. If necessary, the State would use its power of eminent domain to condemn property in order to insure both reasonable land prices and a site of sufficient size and contiguity. The Commission felt that this program would apply the principle of urban renewal to raw land at the fringe of metropolitan areas.

The second program aimed at aiding private developers of large land areas. The Commission had observed that such "community builders" were not likely to offer houses at less than $20,000, a figure which seemed to result chiefly from the high cost of facilities required to launch their ventures. It appeared that low interest-rate, long-term loans from either State or Federal government sources might induce developers to make housing available for lower-income families, especially to those working in or near new communities.

In the course of the Commission's work, several University of California professors, acting as consultants to the Commission, asked me to join them in conversations with the Ford Foundation. The basic question was what, if anything, the Foundation should be doing about the kinds of issues raised by the Commission. The professors argued that the Foundation should expand its already existing urban concerns to include the study of new development at the edges of a metropolis, as well as that of action in the central city. As mentioned earlier, the Community Development Project subsequently was approved by the Foundation, and I joined it as director in early 1964, and Marshall Kaplan as assistant director later that year.

The Proposal

The study was not to be merely an abstract analysis of metropolitan growth, but an "exercise in full-scale civic experimentation." The Proposal began:

> The primary purpose of the program is to develop and test techniques which may be used by the public and private agencies to achieve more desirable patterns of metropolitan growth and expansion in California. . . . Innovation in urban design, finance, political structure, and social institutions may be required to achieve communities which balance these considerations. The project will undertake to identify and evaluate such innovations and to organize a full-scale demonstration, whether of an entire community or selected elements.

No one involved believed that one or two demonstrations would solve all the problems listed in the proposal. But we did believe there was a gap between the understanding of these problems and the institutional framework that now dealt with them—and that innovation was needed to close the gap.

One stimulus behind the Proposal was the emergence of a group of developers this book will call "community builders"—who were possibly the key to implementing this project. From preliminary interviews with operating and prospective community builders came a working definition of the community builder: *an owner of a large, contiguous parcel of land (2500 acres or more) who aims to apply the best known techniques of planning to develop industrial, commercial, residential, and public facilities, as well as amenities not normally found in new suburban developments.*

Out of these interviews came the six-member "Developer Group" (see Figure 1), each of whom met our definition of a community builder with a community in some stage of planning or operation; all were in California.[2] Later—after a visit to Washington and Baltimore—I included also the communities of Columbia (developed by Community Research and Development Company, managed by James Rouse and Company) and Reston (developed by Robert Simon, both of which offered valuable material for this book.[3] Our extensive interviews with developers led us to begin to doubt the usefulness of a demonstration. The Developers Group, however, saw themselves engaging in a new, exciting kind of business and planning. Certain areas worthy of intensive study were suggested— such as the market, political jurisdiction, investment—which contributed to the substance of this book.

The Book

As I have sketched above, the Housing Commission Report and the original Project Proposal were based on the assumption that poverty, racial separation, and fiscal inequity were exacerbated by imperfections and inadequacies in the housing market —that the poor in general and Negroes in particular had little or no access to housing in new suburbs. It seemed to follow that these problems could be attacked by intervention, particularly directed at large-scale developments. But as Kaplan and I read more, worked with those conducting research, and talked with developers, we began to have doubts about these assumptions. Why should the poor, and Negroes, move out of older areas where housing is less expensive and where more jobs for which they qualify may be available? Were there not cultural and social forces at work which would limit the effectiveness of attempts to intervene? Is the growing percentage of nonwhites in central cities such an unmitigated evil for them

---

[2] It seemed reasonable to concentrate analysis in the state which seemed likely to have nearly half the new communities in the nation. Appendix I is a list of most U.S. developments which might be termed new communities.

[3] See Chapter 4, Sections II and III.

or society as a whole? What was lacking in recently built suburbs which new communities or even new towns could provide? Such questions seemed to call for much more thought than had been given them by both of us earlier, or by those who were ready with simple prescriptions.

On another level, we began to question our whole approach to urban affairs. During the Project we lectured to planning students at several universities; few of them knew much about what was going on, or why, in their fields of study; they lacked any precise, factual knowledge which would orient them in understanding the behavior and characteristics of the institutions and individuals who are active in development, and urban affairs.

In the thought and research which have gone into this book, then, we have tried to find out, and then explain, what is going on (and why) before proposing grand solutions. Description and analysis of the new communities has been more important, in fact, than prescription about them.

On the other hand, this book does contain certain conclusions about public policy as well as about the procedures of developers. It is ironic, and somewhat embarassing, for both of us now to find it necessary to criticize the proposal for Federal loans to community builders. Both of us had joined in supporting the idea as a recommendation in the California Commission Report. Kaplan coauthored the initial proposal when he was with the HHFA in 1964, and I supported the legislation in testimony before Congress.

All of this notwithstanding, we ask only to be judged on the basis of our success or failure in describing and evaluating the real work, in stating our own values, and in examining the conclusions to which we came.

EDWARD P. EICHLER

San Francisco, California
August, 1966

Acknowledgments

A GREAT MANY people helped us in this project and in writing the book. It is impossible to acknowledge all of them, but the following people deserve special thanks: Louis Winnick and Paul Ylvysaker of the Ford Foundation, which financed the project; John Dyckman, Director of the Center for Planning and Development Research at Berkeley, who advised us and frequently disagreed but always encouraged us to follow our own path; Melvin Webber, who gave much time and valuable counsel throughout the project; Martin Myerson, formerly Dean of the College of Environmental Design at Berkeley, now President of the State University of New York at Buffalo, who first suggested we write a book; Herbert Gans, whose work on Levittown and advice on field interviewing proved invaluable; William Wheaton, whose criticism was severe but frequently helpful; Harris Dienstfrey, who edited the first draft, and Marie-Ann Seabury, who did the final editing; all the members of the Developer Group, who gave so much of their time and information about their projects, but especially James Rouse of Columbia and Raymond Watson of Irvine; Nathan Glazer and Alan Temko, who made valuable comments on early drafts; Carl Werthman, Ted Dienstfrey, Jerry Mandel, Stanley Scott, Sherman Maisel, Alvin Zelver, Richard Raymond, and Wallace Smith, on whose research this book is partly based; Emily Marlin, the project secretary, who put up with the frequently absurd demands of the authors and who somehow steered the project through the administrative mazes of the University of California; and last and most importantly, our wives, Barbara Kaplan and Doris Eichler, who contributed enormously with their patience and understanding.

Contents

List of Illustrations

List of Tables

DEVELOPERS' GROUP COMMUNITY DEVELOPMENT PROJECT

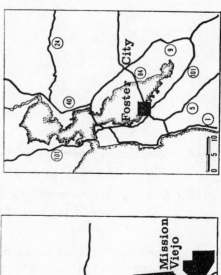

SAN FRANCISCO

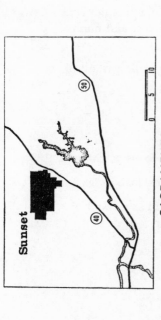

SACRAMENTO

LOS ANGELES

FIGURE 1. Community development projects of the Developer Group.

CHAPTER 1

Planning and the Critique
of Urban Development

AMERICANS have always been ambivalent about cities and about the life of big cities in particular. At its outset, and throughout its great period of western settlement, the country regarded itself as a garden—the garden of the world—even though its settlement was being carried forward by the railroad. And even though the onset of industrialism and the growth of the cities transformed the garden of the world into a land of machine-produced plenty, mechanical agents of change have always been seen somehow as alien presences.[1] This has been especially true for intellectuals, or at least most consistently and articulately so. From Jefferson to Emerson to Dewey—whose philosophy in a sense celebrates the pluralism of American urban life—the basic attitude toward cities can be summarized by John Dewey's statement: "Unless local communal life can be restored, the public cannot resolve its most urgent problem to find and identify itself."

Such general intellectual discontent has taken increasingly specific form in the writings and work of urban critics and planners who have insisted that the existing patterns of urban development lack meaning and order, and destroy community. Taken together, their work forms a critique whose adherents by now range from the academy to the mass media to government. Because of its broad and articulate base of support, this critique has strongly influenced the development of the new communities. It has helped create an atmosphere in which the

---

[1] See Leo Marx, *The Machine in the Garden* (New York: Oxford University Press, 1964) for a penetrating discussion of the pastoral ideal in America, both in the general consciousness and in American literature—and how this ideal responded to the coming of the machine.

1

objectives of the new communities are seen as matters of public concern. More directly, the critique has provided many of the builders with the terms they use to express what they are doing and why. Most significantly, it has provided several of them with one of the ruling motives behind their activity.

The critique of urban development thus is part of the ground out of which the new communities have grown. This chapter takes a look at its foremost features, chiefly as seen through the words of its creators.

Ebenezer Howard and the Garden City

Modern America thought about the defects of contemporary urban life and the social organizations in which these defects could be righted, begins with an Englishman. Ebenezer Howard, writing in the last decade of the nineteenth century, based his view of contemporary urban life on an analysis of the waste and disorganization which the industrial revolution had brought to Europe's major cities. Howard saw urban centers growing larger and larger and felt that this growth would intensify all the problems of the city and make life there less and less humane. In his book, *Tomorrow: A Peaceful Path to Real Reform,*[2] first published in 1898, Howard proposed that the English government establish a series of small, self-sufficient towns under public control. The population of each was to approximate 30,000. By owning the land, the town could profit from the appreciation in land value and thus finance local services. The towns would be connected by transportation systems to the country's major urban center, London, and would be designed to catch London's "over-spill." Each town would be protected from encroachment (and prevented from expanding) by a permanent greenbelt circumscribing its borders.

Howard did not conceive of the new towns he proposed as elements that in themselves would right the defects of city life.

---

[2] The book was later slightly revised and published in a second edition with the title changed to *Garden Cities of Tomorrow* (London: S. Sonnenschein, 1902).

Rather he saw a symbiotic relationship between city and suburb:

There are in reality not only, as is so constantly assumed, two alternatives—town life and country life—but a third alternative in which all the advantages of the most energetic and active town life, with all the beauty and delight of the country, may be secured in perfect combination; and the certainty of being able to live this life will be the magnet which will produce the effect for which we are all striving—the spontaneous movement of the people from our crowded cities to the bosom of our kindly mother earth, at once the source of life, of happiness, of wealth, and of power.[3]

Howard's concept of the Garden City found many adherents in the United States, one of the earliest being Patrick Geddes. In *Cities in Evolution,* written a decade after Howard's work, Geddes took the Garden-City concept and proposed such towns as part of regional plans. The first realization of Howard's concept in England came in 1904 with the developments of Letchwork (designed by Barry Parker and Raymond Unwin) and Welwyn (Unwin). The concept as modified by Geddes did not become a reality in the United States for almost another thirty years. During this period, it was kept alive by the work of the Regional Planning Association, a New York organization formed to encourage area-wide planning. Its brilliant list of members included Lewis Mumford (who had been a student of Geddes), Stuart Chase, Catherine Bauer, Clarence Stein, and Henry Wright.

With the advent of the depression, the Federal government (as well as many private, local groups) made a concerted effort to shift people from cities to adjoining rural areas; the government established over one hundred developments, most of them intended as experiments in non-urban (in a manner of speaking, even anti-urban) living. Their prime purpose was either to attract people "back to the land" or to encourage subsistence farming.

During Roosevelt's second term, the government's Resettlement Administration began to develop three new communities

---

[3] Ebenezer Howard, *Garden Cities of Tomorrow* (London: Faber and Faber, 1914), pp. 45–46.

on the basis of Geddes' modification of Howard. These communities were the "greenbelt" towns: Greenbelt, Maryland; Greenhills, Cincinnati; and Greendale, Milwaukee. With the exception of Stein's Radburn, they constitute the only major attempt to establish English-style garden cities in America. The towns were each to have had a population of up to 10,000 and a full range of community facilities—schools, hospitals, cultural centers, and so forth. The Resettlement Administration, and particularly its Administrator, Rexford Tugwell, saw the towns as a way to meet the challenges of suburban growth and, at the same time, provide lower-income families with new and better housing.

With the end of the depression, and the start of the war, this bold experiment in public planning came to an end. The greenbelt towns were never completed and were engulfed by subsequent urbanization. Yet even as they stand today, shadows of an unrealized hope, they remain a testimonial to Tugwell's far-reaching vision.

The Regional Mess

The urban-development critique, considered as a whole, is a recoil of horror and outrage at what is seen as urbanization run wild. The language often runs to science-fiction images of devastation and monstrous growths. A typical example comes from the California architect, Richard Neutra, in an analysis with the dark title, *Survival Through Design*. Neutra asks: "Must we remain victims, strangled and suffocated by our own design which has surrounded us with man-devouring metropolises, drab small towns manifesting a lack of order devastating to the soul, blighted countrysides along railroad tracks and highways, studded with petty mere utility structures shaded by telephone poles and scented by gasoline fumes?"[4] Similarly, Lewis Mumford speaks of the failure to divide its [the me-

---

[4] Richard Neutra, *Survival Through Design* (New York: Oxford University Press, 1954).

tropolis'] social chromosomes and split up into new cells, each bearing some portion of the original inheritance, the city continues to grow inorganically, indeed cancerously, by a continuous breaking down of old tissues, and an overgrowth of formless tissue.[5] Probably the most specific formulation of the development critique's basic response to the contemporary situation comes from Peter Blake's book, *God's Own Junkyard*, written in 1964. Blake, editor of *Architectural Forum*, says: ". . . we are about to turn this beautiful inheritance [the American landscape] into the biggest slum on the face of the earth. 'The mess that is man-made America,' as a British magazine has called it, is a disgrace of such vast proportions that only a concerted national effort can hope to return physical America to the community of civilized nations."[6]

According to the critique, nothing escapes the brutal marks of the urbanization process, which begins in the old central cities. In the words of Senator Harrison Williams of New Jersey: "The impact of this decentralization of downtown areas is plain to see. Business wilts in the traffic congestion, property values sink, tax revenue declines, slums multiply and the need for a larger urban renewal program intensifies."[7] The great functions of the city are also seriously weakened. From another national magazine, *House and Home*: "Suburban sprawl negates and frustrates the purpose of cities which is to let more people live and work close together and so utilize and enjoy the maximum efficiency of community facilities and community enterprises, with easy access and cheap distribution."[8]

Not only the city suffers, but the area around it as well. Between the city and the suburb, aesthetic damage is coupled with a new kind of emotional pressure. Senator Williams again: "Frenzied traffic makes driving an obstacle race, and the greed

---

[5] Lewis Mumford, *The City in History* (New York: Harcourt, Brace, and World, 1961), p. 543.

[6] Peter Blake, *God's Own Junkyard* (New York: Holt, Rinehart, and Winston, 1964), p. 8.

[7] Senator Harrison Williams, U.S. Senate Committee on Banking and Currency, 87th Congress, 1st Session, *Hearings*, Housing Legislation of 1961.

[8] "Land," *House and Home*, XVIII, 2 (August 1960), p. 114.

of the subdividers disfigures the city's natural beauty."[9] There is also economic waste. From a brochure describing the situation in California in 1962, "California, Going, Going . . ." issued by California Tomorrow, a non-profit educational institution: ". . . this state's supremely attractive resources of land, air and water are being defiled by disorderly, unsightly intrusions of subdivisions, cars, roads, parking spaces, sewage, exhaust, strip development, suburbs—sloppy, sleasy, slovenly, slipshod semi-cities."[10] The waste and economic inefficiency extend even to the developments. William Whyte, one of the earliest students of contemporary suburbia, details the point in his study, *The Exploding Metropolis*: "Where the new developments are scattered at random in the outlaying areas, the costs of providing services becomes excruciating. There is not only the cost of running sewers and water mains and storm drains out to Happy Acres but much more road, per family served, has to be paved and maintained. . . . Sprawl also means low volume utility operation for the amount of installation involved."[11]

But what of the developments themselves? What are they like? And how do their residents fare? The critique sees no relief here either. A best-seller on conditions in the new suburbia, John Keats' *The Crack in the Picture Window*, describes the life it offers in these terms: ". . . a housing development cannot be called a community, for that word implies a balanced society of men, women and children wherein work and pleasure are found and the needs of all the society's members are several. Housing developments offer no employment and as a general rule lack recreational areas, churches, schools or other cohesive influences."[12]

E. A. Gutkind, discussing suburbia in his book, *The Expanding Environment*, summons up all the apocalyptic horror of the urban-development critique in the following statement:

---

[9] *Ibid.*

[10] Samuel E. Wood and Alfred E. Heller, *California, Going, Going . . .* (Sacramento, Calif.: California Tomorrow, 1962).

[11] William Whyte, *The Exploding Metropolis* (Garden City, N.Y.: Doubleday, Anchor Books, 1958), p. 122.

[12] John Keats, *The Crack in the Picture Window* (Boston: Mifflin, 1957), Introduction, p. xvi.

"The last vestiges of a community have disappeared. They are hardly anything else than an agglomeration of innumerable and isolated details, of human atoms, and rows of boxes, called houses, interspersed between the industries. It is a total victory of a laissez faire insensibility and recklessness over organic growth and even over organized development."[13]

How Did it Happen?

The urban-development critique lists many factors that have contributed to this deplorable situation—among them, rising levels of income, population growth, and the increased mobility provided by the automobile. But to this group of critics, none of these factors seem fundamental; what brought the country to its present pass was speculation and misguided, piecemeal Federal policies. The writings of the urban critique strike this note again and again. Typical references can be gleaned from Senator Williams' testimony, Arthur Gallion's *The Urban Pattern*, William Whyte's *The Exploding Metropolis*, and so on. Probably the most concise formulation of the argument appears in Peter Blake's *God's Own Junkyard*.

Suburbia got that way for two simple reasons: first, because the developers who built it are, fundamentally, no different from manufacturers of any other mass produced product: they standardize the product, package it, arrange for rapid distribution and easy financing and sell it off the shelf as fast as they can. And, second, because the Federal government, through FHA and other agencies set up to cope with the serious housing shortages that arose after World War II, has imposed a bureaucratic straight jacket on the design of most new houses, on the placement of houses on individual lots, on landscaping, on street planning, and on just about everything else that gives suburbia its "wasteland" appearance.[14]

In short, the disastrous sprawl of the past twenty years is seen as the product of the merchant builder and the government bureaucrat together, each in his own way responding only to the immediate needs of the moment.

---

[13] As quoted in Keats, *op. cit.*, p. 176.
[14] Blake, *op. cit.*, p. 17.

What Is the Cure?

There are any number of proposals in the different writings of the urban-development critique as to how future urbanization should proceed and the nature of goals at which it should aim. Here is a small sampling from as many authors as there are quotations. It will be clear that they are all part of one extended discussion.

We are going to have to relate the adequate house of our future to the community in which it will stand.[15]

. . . the metropolis should be "imageable." That is, it should be visually vivid and well structured; its component parts should be easily recognized and easily interrelated. This objective would encourage the use of intensive centers, variety, sharp gain, and a differentiated but well patterned flow system.[16]

We could begin to establish and enforce statewide standards for the location and development of our cities to make sure that they are reasonably compact, widely separated by open space, served by suitable transportation, and balanced enough to minimize the need for long distance cross commuting, whether to jobs or to leisure time facilities.[17]

In short, it makes eminently good economic sense for suburbia to encourage a mixture of building types, if only to reduce the cost of public schools. Quite obviously, it makes just as good economic sense to encourage the concentration of buildings on the one hand, and the open park land on the other, so as to reduce the length of roads and utilities, and the cost of policing or maintaining them.[18]

Common to all these proposals is one central idea: that future developments should be conceived in terms of wholes—that they be determined on the basis of essential physical,

---

[15] Keats, *op. cit.*, p. 184.
[16] Kevin Lynch, "The Pattern of the Metropolis," Daedalus, XC, 1, Journal of the American Academy of Arts and Sciences, (Winter 1961), p. 94.
[17] Samuel E. Wood and Alfred E. Heller, *Phantom Cities of California*, (Sacramento, Calif.: California Tomorrow, 1963), pp. 65–66.
[18] Blake, *op. cit.*, p. 19.

social, economic, and human needs. Future development, in other words, must be thoroughly planned.

To the urban-development critique the past twenty years has been a period of pernicious individualism and destructive chaos. Against these forces, the critique opposes the rational mind and its ability to plan. To the critique, it is planning—executed from a sufficiently high level of comprehensiveness—that will build Utopia.

This relentless and seemingly thorough-going critique was bound to influence men whose general interest in civic affairs was already high. For owners of large parcels of land, such as Janss and Irvine (developers of Janss/Conejo and Irvine Ranch, respectively); for inheritors of wealth accumulated through real-estate ventures such as Robert Simon (the developer of Reston), and for some who had earned their own fortunes in a field related to real estate, as had James Rouse (the developer of Columbia)—the chance to shape a new life style in suburbia was irresistible. At the same time, such men are products of a culture which esteems those who make a profit. Thus, they would not just "create better communities" but would earn money doing it. The great aim of the community builders is to prove that the profit motive can be harnessed to meet head on the deficiencies exposed by the critique of urban development.

As the planning for new communities proceeded, however, conflicts arose between the goals of the planners and the profit motive. Most often, the conflict arose over how to deal with the planners' enemy, the automobile. In his book, *The Heart of our Cities*, architect Victor Gruen, whose firm drew the plans of at least six new communities, describes his concept of the properly designed metropolis:

> The low densities in the neighborhoods (50 persons per gross acre) are considerably higher than those we find in our sprawling suburban areas . . .
> Within each of the neighborhoods, within the community centers, the town centers, the city centers and the various nuclei of Metrocenter, there will be a pattern of pedestrian walks and plazas, and this pattern will extend into the green areas surrounding them, in order to connect various nuclei with each other . . .

Local vehicular roads and highways . . . related to each one of the nuclei, will be established as loop roads surrounding each nucleus and connecting up to car storage facilities located on the fringe of each nucleus in the form of underground or multiple-deck garages. In a neighborhood, for example, garages will not be attached to every residence.[19]

Gruen, like many other urban critics and planners, apparently believes either that most suburbanites do not really want to rely on automobiles or that they should be forced to adopt another style of life. But confronted with early plans for relatively high-density neighborhoods in which parking was separated from the individual dwelling, community builders consistently decided that most of their prospective customers would continue to demand low-density, detached houses with attached garages.

What underlies this conflict seems to be the planners' antipathy for the American middle class and a yearning for aristocratic taste and values: "All this [suburbia]," writes Lewis Mumford, "is a far cry from the aristocratic enjoyment of visual space that provided the late Baroque city with open squares and circles and long vistas for carriage drives down tree lined avenues."[20] The businessmen undertaking new communities may share this view, but time and again they have been forced to remind themselves and their planners that this very middle class is the market to which their project must appeal.

Proponents of planning have come more and more to see planning as a dynamic process, which enables decision-makers to be better prepared to cope with exigencies as they arise. Too often the planning process for new communities has been the opposite. It has been an attempt to bind the community builder and the occupants of new communities to a preconceived set of notions about what suburban life ought to be. Much of this book will illustrate the difficulties which arise under such conditions.

---

19 Victor Gruen, *The Heart of Our Cities* (New York: Simon 1964), pp. 274, 277–278.
20 Mumford, *op cit.*, p. 503.

CHAPTER 2

From Frontier to Megalopolis

LAND SPECULATION and land development have always been a part of American economic experience. Unlike the populace of many nations, most Americans have always accepted the notion that the settling of new areas is a legitimate enterprise for monetary gain. This chapter is a thumbnail sketch of the historical patterns of urban growth in America, of the forces which determined the nature of that growth, and of the institutions which attempted to profit from it.

The owner, trader, or developer of land has not shaped America; rather, his behavior has been a response to such forces as national policies, changes in technology, social and cultural factors, shifts in income distribution, or rises in total income. None of these forces were stimulated, nor were any policies advanced deliberately to produce a particular form of urban settlement. Particularly in the nineteenth century, national policy was to settle the continent and to industrialize, in whatever way possible. Whether land developers reacted well in helping achieve these ends, in terms either of their own interest or that of society, is difficult to say; the fact that theirs *was* a response, and the *nature* of the response are the subject of this chapter.

The First Phase: Grab-Bag Days

Originally land meant status and nobility. In general, the larger the land holding the higher the status and the grander the nobility. Even before the Revolutionary War—which ended feudal carryovers such as entail (limiting the inheritance of an estate to a single line of heirs) and primogeniture (succession by law to the first-born)—colonists were acquiring large blocks of land. This they did primarily through grants from the king. Land very quickly had become a kind of blank check to be cashed as the country grew. Land grabbing became the avocation of many of the country's most prominent citizens—including Washington, Patrick Henry, the Lees, and the Masons.

The Revolution dampened speculative spirit, but once the war was won and a new nation born, land was sought again with even more vigor. In 1783, Silas Deane in a letter to a friend, noted quite correctly: "If we review the rise and progress of private fortunes in America, we shall find that a very small proportion of them has arisen or been acquired by commerce, compared with those made by the prudent purchases and management of lands."[1]

For the most part, the policies of the fledgling national government and of the states encouraged the activities of land speculators. The end of the war left states with vast areas of unsettled land which they regarded as a source of tender to pay off accumulated debts; many states issued land warrants to soldiers. The new government similarly used its land to meet payments on the national debt. Speculators eagerly sought land warrants and formed companies to raise money for their acquisition. These companies secured the services of individuals to identify good parcels of land, and they also hired jobbers to corner the necessary warrants. Large contiguous areas were much more saleable than isolated lots.

The states themselves had various land claims and, as a means of settling peacefully the disputes that arose, all land west of the Alleghanies was ceded to the Federal government. On the basis of this land, the government legislatively created the Northwest Territory, by enacting the Northwest Ordinance of 1787. After this Congress was beseiged for grants of vast tracts. Under the Ordinance, land was laid out in townships six miles square and in sections of 640 acres. The government

---

[1] A. M. Sakolski, *The Great American Land Bubble* (New York: Harper and Brothers, 1932), p. 29.

sold the land at a minimum of one 640-acre section for $1 per acre, payable within a year.

To all parties in these transactions, land was merely something that could be converted into large sums of money if only one had enough of it and could move it quickly enough. Land was the way one made a fortune (or lost everything one had), or it was the way governmental bodies paid off their debts. But it was something that had to be improved in any way before becoming a desirable commodity.

1800–1837: From the Homesteader to the Railroad

By the turn of the century, there were two conflicting attitudes toward national land policy. On one side were the individuals who argued that land should be used to fill the Federal treasury, and that the only way to do this was to sell it in large blocks. On the other side were those who argued that since the United States was, and ought to be, a nation of homesteaders, land speculation and large lots were evils that weakened the well-being of the country. Though the argument went on for some fifty years national policy, for the most part, backed the homesteader.

After 1800, the minimum acreage for sale was reduced from 640 to 320 acres, with a price of $2 per acre payable over a five-year period. By 1820, the minimum acreage was reduced to 80, and the price reduced to $1.25.

The first great burst of speculation fever had abated. By 1800 several of the large companies had collapsed (partly because of the government's cheap land policies), and large amounts of land reverted back to the states. At this point, speculation entered a new phase—speculators became "town creators." They hired agents to stimulate migration from Europe, and opened land offices in the East to sell lots to the immigrants in new, "planned" communities. Promoters outdid each other in painting their venture as God's gift to humanity and as a cure-all for the urban ills already being felt. "A new way of life for Europe's downtrodden masses"; "Escape from the congestion of New York, Boston or Philadelphia"; "Climate, fertile soil." Utopia beckoned if the buyer would but listen.

The actual improvements in most of these areas were quite minor, intended only to make the land appear attractive as cheaply as possible so it could be disposed of as quickly as possible. Speculation, not serious development, still was the guiding principle. Of the many new towns promoted, only a few were successful—though among them one finds the names of Bath (New York), Cincinnati, Cleveland, and Marietta (Ohio).

Transactions in raw land, in city and town lots, and in non-urban areas, continued to be prevalent. There was even some interest in suburban development for high-income families.[2]

During the 1830's speculation again rose to a fever pitch. So-called "rag" money—notes issued from wildcat banks—was used to procure public lands. Jackson's "specie circuler" of 1836 effectively blunted this activity by ordering that only hard currency—gold, silver, or land scrip—could be accepted by land offices. But the respite was brief; with the advent of the railroad and with the cry of "Go West, young Man!" the urge to acquire land became more powerful than ever.

Midcentury: Manifest Destiny and the Open West

By 1841, the country was clearly moving toward a national policy that favored a quick settlement of the West. The government, however, continued to support the individual home-steader as against the large land speculator. The Pre-emption Act of 1841 gave squatters the right to buy up to 160 acres of "their claim." The Homestead Act of 1862 gave the squatter complete ownership of 160 acres if he had lived there and cul-tivated them for five years; this gradually was reduced to

---

[2] In 1836 the New Brighton Company made plans to develop Staten Island, N. Y., as an upper-class enclave. The panic of 1837 and the de-pression that followed put an end to that attempt.

three years. Later legislation turned full circle and permitted individuals to buy the land at a nominal price instead of meeting a residence requirement.

The railroad, of course, was the crucial force in western settlement. By midcentury the government was awarding giant land grants directly to private railroad-building companies. The first major grant went to the Illinois Central Railroad in 1850—2,600,000 acres, which included alternate sections of land up to six miles in depth on either side of the proposed tracks. The government gave its most mammoth grant (47,000,000 acres) to Jay Cooke's Northern Pacific Railroad.

In many instances railroad companies actually looked to the land rather than to the operations of the road, to be their major source of profit. They sold land which was part of the future railroad's right of way to speculators and town jobbers. Existing towns and cities fought to be selected as terminal points or junctions, offering concessions to the railroads if their individual locale was chosen.

During this period of speculation and expansion the first serious efforts were made to plan and build whole towns. Dozens of private companies were created by the sale of stock, and throughout the eastern portion of the nation and in Europe, they hunted for potential residents. As one company wrote: "We will seek to gather into localities, communities of emigrants, taking some from every class and sending them out in a body to establish a town or village of their own."

The railroads were major developers of the new towns. Jay Cooke, founder of the Northern Pacific, attempted to establish towns all along the railroad's right of way.[3] Each Northern

---

[3] Years before, Cooke had bought 19,000 acres of rich pine land in the area now known as Duluth. Cooke envisioned the area as a great port and railroad terminal. He sold most of his lots to Civil War veterans and Europeans. The depression of 1873 (which ultimately caused Cooke's departure from the Northern Pacific) proved near fatal. The population of the town fell from 5,000 to 2,500. After the Northern Pacific was reorganized, the railroad finally reached the West Coast, and sales of lots picked up. They provided Cooke with his remaining major source of income. He had lived to see his vision come true.

Pacific land office displayed model prefabricated homes which cost from between $200 to $1,000 to build. The company in addition offered extremely liberal credit terms to lot buyers.

But between the time of the government's distribution of free land to homesteaders, which cut into the potential market, and the crash of 1873, the life chances of the towns were fairly slim. Though the railroads continued to create towns, few succeeded. The competition of free government land proved too severe. Though by 1900 the railroads had received 183,000,000 acres from the government, some 600,000 farmers had received grants totalling nearly half that amount, 80,000,000 acres.

⌐ During the latter part of the century, large industrial concerns also made several efforts to establish new towns. Most of the companies were mainly interested in securing a stable labor market. Although a number of the companies were motivated also by a paternalistic desire to improve the lot of the worker, their paternalism usually bordered on the dictatorial. As a rule the companies completely controlled the lives and fortunes of both the town and its residents, serving as combination landlord, city manager, and employer. The town's housing units were either sold outright or leased to the employees.⌐ Stores and other service facilities usually belonged to the company.[4] The founding of company towns has continued well into the twentieth century.[5] Curiously, despite the monopolistic nature of these communities, most were not profiitable, perhaps because they had only one industry and so were subject to a high degree of economic instability. Bureau of Labor Statistics suggests that the gross return on their aggregate investment approximated only 8.3 per cent.

---

[4] A typical company town, one of the first, was Hopedale, near Milford, Massachusetts. Originally established in 1841 as a Christian Socialist experiment, it was taken over in 1856 by the Draper Corporation, which provided housing for the workers employed in the Company's cotton machine plant. Typically, the company owned most of the land within the corporate limits of the development.

[5] Several prominent examples are Gary, Indiana, established in 1906 by U.S. Steel; Kingsport, Tennessee, established in 1915 by the Kuppert Farms, Inc.; Kohler, Wisconsin, established in 1916 by the Kohler Co.; and Chicopee, Georgia, established in 1924 by the Chicopee Manufacturing Company.

By the end of the nineteenth century, town development had taken its place alongside the aggregation of land as a regular form of speculative enterprise, though it was by no means typical. For the most part, home building still remained a concern of the individual. If a man wanted a new home, either he built it himself or had it built for him. The thought had occurred hardly to anyone that a man might choose a home as he chose, say, a hat—ready made.

1900–1930: Suburbia, the Subdivider, and the Developer

By 1900, 40 per cent of the country's population lived in urban areas. In absolute numbers this was almost ten times the urban population of 1850. To many rural and European migrants, America's cities presented a new way of life, but to many other people—the "older" stock Americans—it had begun to represent a place to escape from when work was finished. To this latter group, the city often seemed a locus for festering crime, for corruption and alien ideas, for blight and slums. As the incomes of these people rose, more and more of them left the city. Technological development helped them—first the train, then the trolley, and finally the automobile. As the transportation network expanded, reducing the costs and difficulties of travel, the potential area of residence around the city and the housing market also expanded. Thus, what at first was a sporadic stroll soon became a march, and was yet to become a flight; the growth of suburbia had begun.

With this development came the land subdivider, a combination of retail land-merchant, promoter, and broker. Like the town jobber and the land speculator, his nineteenth-century predecessors, the subdivider of the early twentieth century was usually not interested in putting up units or in treating the land as a long-term investment. Yet unlike his predecessors, who speculated on locations "destined to be great emporiums of trade, industry, commerce," the subdivider was, so to speak, an urban phenomenon—a figure who focused his activities on meeting the needs of urban residents who wanted to escape the city's ills, actual or imagined.

This sort of land developer operated as follows: he secured a piece of land, usually on the outskirts of already established communities, laid out imaginary lots and streets, and quickly turned to promotion. On occasion, the arrival of a competitor would drive both to put in minimal improvements. Local municipalities were eager to help minimize the subdivider's costs and risk (through such devices as special assessment privileges), for they looked to him to bring growth and prosperity to their areas. Though most subdividers were individual operators, a number of companies and several banks formed to engage in land speculation and to fund subdividing activities. There were also a few syndicates which bought large tracts and held them for future sale to subdividers.

As in the previous century, speculation increased during periods of general economic expansion. During the boom days of the twenties, the production of lots exceeded the immediate market—optimism was the order of the day—and the depression of 1929 left many cities with abortive or under-utilized subdivisions.

The subdivisions and their residents suffered the consequences in the next decade. They were forced to live without proper facilities, because of inadequate and incorrect layout, and over-all poor planning. These deficiencies gave rise to subdivision codes and zoning regulations which in turn helped produce a change in the character of the subdivider during the late thirties. Beyond being a promoter and a speculator, he was forced to become something of a true land developer—at least to the extent of installing a minimum level of facilities.

Throughout these decades, there was a wide variety of efforts (though their absolute number was small) at planning communities. The most extensive of these efforts in the first half of the twentieth century were the large-scale suburban subdivisions planned mostly for middle- and upper-income families—Roland Park in Baltimore (founded in 1890 and still standing today as an example of good physical planning); Country Club District in Kansas City (1905); Forest Hills Gardens in Long Island (planned in 1908 by the renowned landscape architect, F. L. Olmstead); Shaker Heights in Cleveland (intriguing, among other reasons, for the railroad built by the developers, the Van Sweringen brothers, to attract residents); Palos Verdes Estates in Los Angeles (1923); and, perhaps most famous of all, Radburn, New Jersey. Radburn started out to be a full-fledged new town quite comparable to those of the English new-town movement. It was founded in 1927 by the City Housing Corporation of New York, a nonprofit group which wanted to create a relatively self-contained community. But the depression thwarted the dream of the developers by making it impossible for them to establish a strong industrial base in the town. Radburn is now a middle- and upper-income subdivision with 788 units (638 for single families, 50 duplex units, and 100 apartments). Radburn's noted planners (Clarence Stein, and architect Henry Wright) used the development to promote the concepts of the superblock and the cul-de-sac.

Other attempts to bridge the gap between minimal subdivision and full-scale development were made by a number of individuals who acquired land, subdivided it, installed improvements, and either built units for sale themselves or worked in close coordination with contract builders and emerging groups of large-home builders. Again the intended market was generally middle- and upper-income families, and many of the subdivisions included such recreational facilities as golf courses and swimming pools. Though a number of philanthropic individuals and groups attempted to provide relief from the harshness of urban life for minority and lower-income households, their efforts remained completely apart from the mainstream of development activity.[6]

---

[6] Some examples are the Amalgamated Clothing Workers Union Cooperative, the Paul Laurance Dunbar Apartments (John Rockefeller), and the Marshall Field Garden Apartments, all created in the 1920's.

After World War II: The Merchant Builder and the Community Builder

At the end of World War II, the sudden release of a housing demand that had been accumulating since the early thirties brought with it the most important of all the types of developers that have passed in review—the merchant builder. The housing demand swelled with the rising income of the population, programs of the Federal Housing Agency and the Veterans Administration, increasing automobile ownership, and massive road building.

In 1938, according to Miles Colean's study, *American Housing*, there had been 70,000 to 80,000 urban home builders who constructed one or more units annually. The average number of units per builder was 3.5. Less than 20 per cent of the builders put up four or more units a year, and 2 per cent (accounting for over 30 per cent of the units built) put up 25 or more units. Building organizations were small, under-capitalized, locally based, and many supplemented their income with other business activities.[7]

Even in the largest cities, more than half of the builders took out permits to build only one house each inside the city limits. In some cases they may have built homes outside the city or may have done other kinds of construction work. In many instances they were owner builders, deriving their income from sources other than the construction industry. A large number were subcontractors or construction craftsmen, dependent on construction activities for the bulk of their incomes, but not solely as general contractors or speculative builders.[8]

The situation after the War changed all this. It made the production of houses an industry. From 1945 to 1960, about 1.3 million units were produced annually. Four per cent of the

---

[7] Miles Colean, *American Housing* (New York: Twentieth Century Fund, 1947).

[8] *Builders of One-family Houses in 72 Cities*, Serial No. R1151, Bureau of Labor Statistics, 1940.

firms accounted for 45 per cent of this production. The largest of the companies produced from 2,000 to 3,000 units a year.

But it is not quantity alone which separates the prewar and postwar builders; rather, new techniques made possible the incredible production of the postwar years. In 1947 *Fortune* magazine put the problem facing builders this way: "The search for reform in the housebuilding business becomes primarily a search for large scale operations. Efficient house production requires firms big enough to mobilize capital and organize production in systematic, repetitive operations."[9]

What set the merchant builder apart was the fact that he merged together in a single firm the processes of land purchase, site improvements (utilities, streets, sidewalks), house construction, and merchandising. Before 1945, each of these operations usually was carried out by a different firm. Merging them permitted greater efficiency. But such efficiency was economically worthwhile only under conditions in which the rate of sale in one location was sufficiently high (usually 100 or more units per year). In other words, the emergence of the merchant builder was a direct response to the conditions following the war.

In the fifties, the country's urban area expanded by nearly 5,000,000 acres—primarily through growth at the city's edges, where the merchant builders worked. The face of the country was transformed—developments, freeways, giant shopping centers sprang up as if overnight. Though it had begun decades before, a whole new mode of life, suburbia, seemed to come into being all at once. Industry and people had moved out, but they had not moved out together—and the result was that many different kinds of communities appeared to ring the city. The suburbs extracted singly economic and social functions which had existed side by side in the cities.

Almost as quickly as the suburbs, a vivid vocabulary of dismay and anger arose to describe their effects: "slurb," "sprawl," "scatteration." It is one of the purposes of this book

---

[9] "The Industry Capitalism Forgot," *Fortune*, XXXVI, 2 (August 1947), pp. 61–67, 167–170.

to reopen the discussion of whether such language is indeed appropriate to the random, unplanned, market-oriented growth of suburbia; it has seemed so to many critics. They have argued that the merchant builder has had only one concern, money, and that in the name of money he has viciously scarred the countryside, exacerbated all the old problems of the city, and created a host of new ones. The development he engendered completely disregarded human or social needs. At the end of the fifties, the community builder stepped forward hoping to prove there was an alternative—and a profitable one at that.

CHAPTER 3

Breaking Ground for the New Communities

THE URBAN-DEVELOPMENT critique (see Chapter 1) gave new communities part of their philosophical reason for being. The existence of large tracts of land under single ownership, the rapid conversion of agricultural land to urban use, and the action of government to aid in this conversion provided, especially in California, the other necessary condition for community building—that the operation could be profitable.

Since this entire book in a sense is an extended definition of "community builders" and "new communities," a preliminary description is in order. Technically, land subdivision is simply the process of dividing a given parcel of land into two or more parts, each of which can then be sold. In the following discussion, we will refer to land development as the process both of subdividing land into smaller parcels and of installing basic site improvements—streets, sidewalks, water, power, and so on. As we use the term, land development may, but need not, imply the construction of buildings and the installation of leisure-time amenities, such as a swimming pool or golf course. Especially in California, the process of land development, has tended to include house construction and thus produce what is called a "merchant builder."

The principal difference between a subdivision as such and a new community is scale. As a rule, a 1000-acre subdivision is considered very large; but as we shall see, the smallest of the new communities has at least 2,500 acres. Scale is not the only difference. Other differences to be discussed include such matters as the range of facilities proposed or offered, the number of years of projected involvement, and the institutional framework created for the process.

23

A new town, in the European sense, may not be larger than a new community, but it is different in many other respects. The term itself is incorporated into law in Great Britain where the national government passed the New Towns Act in 1947. The principal purpose of this law is to decant population from existing regions or cities. The critical difference between a new town and a new community is in the degree of "self-sufficiency," of each, which means the percentage of the population expected to live and work within the area. This is what most residents of a British new town are expected to do. To achieve this, the government selects and purchases the site, passes regulations preventing additional development beteween the new town and other urban areas, provides housing subsidies, and, most important of all, regulates and induces industry to settle in the town. American new communities—except defense installations, retirement or resort settlements—are within the metropolitan area, receive no government aid to secure industry, therefore are populated largely by resident commuters in the early years, and are not separated from other urban land uses by a governmentally created "greenbelt."

Thus a new community is much less self-sufficient than a new town. A new town is an attempt to break the pattern of urban growth, and at the same time to shift development to different places and to control it. A new community is a way of ordering the business of land development at the fringe of American metropolitan areas.

This chapter is based on the experience in California, and focuses on the chain of events that form the backdrop for such development—population growth, the way the "migrants" used the new land, and the governmental response.

From 1784 to 1848, the year California became a state, the Spanish government rewarded more than a thousand individuals with "ranchos," tracts of land sometimes exceeding 100,000 acres, most of which were in Southern California. By 1870, after 20 years of legal clarification, more than 800 ranchos were recognized by the United States government as valid. Even as late as 1955, they remained only vestiges of vast accumulations of land on which, at best, cattle grazed, oranges grew, and westerns were filmed (Janss/Conejo). But after World War II, the great migrations from farm to city, from east to west, and from central cities to the suburbs, gradually began to offer the prospect that this land might be converted from agricultural to urban (and presumably more valuable) use.

People and Land

In the summer of 1962, a giant neon-punctured billboard on the San Francisco Bay Bridge flashed a minute-by-minute account of California's "battle" to overcome New York's national population lead. Replicas appeared in all parts of the state. Any minute it was going to be No. 1, and all but a few residents viewed the coming victory with pride.

California's population growth has always been an interesting phenomenon. Its rate of growth always has exceeded that of the nation. Between 1950 and 1960 the state's population increased by 48.5 per cent while the growth rate for the nation as a whole was only 18.4 per cent. Most of California's growth has taken place within its metropolitan areas, whose population increased from 2.7 million people in 1920 to 13.6 million in 1960. Between 1950 and 1960, 90 per cent of all the population growth in the state was in metropolitan areas.

Most of this new settlement has not taken the form of increased densities or filling up vacant land within the older cities or sections of the metropolis. Instead it has occurred at the fringes of urban areas, and beyond. Between 1950 and 1960 three times as many people chose to live in suburbs as in the central cities, and four of the states central cities actually lost population.

As the suburbs gained in population, more land was required per person than before. Population per square mile in metropolitan areas went down from 4,786 in 1950 to 4,061 in 1960. This decreasing density resulted from higher rates of automobile ownership, consumer preference for more private space and, in some instances, from local zoning laws which required larger lots for homes and permitted less apartment units per acre.

LOS ANGELES URBANIZATION PATTERN 1950-1960

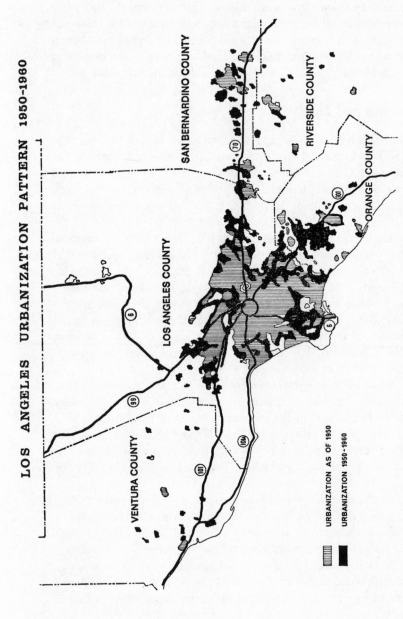

URBANIZATION AS OF 1950

URBANIZATION 1950-1960

VENTURA COUNTY

LOS ANGELES COUNTY

SAN BERNARDINO COUNTY

RIVERSIDE COUNTY

ORANGE COUNTY

FIGURE 2. Los Angeles urbanization pattern, 1950–1960.

Particularly in Los Angeles this consumption of vacant land brought many large holdings to the edge of or even inside the ring of urbanization. The map in Figure 2 illustrates this. It shows the land developed in Los Angeles from 1950 to 1960 and the relationship between some of the new communities now in the planning or operational stage. There are a great many other tracts of 2,500 acres or more not shown which may be yet developed by community builders.

Freeways and New Communities

In 1939, the California Legislature adopted the freeway principle. A freeway is a highway to which the adjoining property does not have the right of access. By 1953, forty-five miles of freeway (parts of the Hollywood, Santa Ana, San Bernardino, and Long Beach freeways) were in operation. In 1959 the Legislature formally adopted a master plan which called for the construction of 12,500 miles of state highways.[1]

In the Los Angeles area (as well as in the rest of the state) the impact of the freeway system on prospective land developers was significant. Population growth with its consumption of land brought people, employment, shopping, and leisure activities closer to large land holdings. Freeways have further reduced (or shortly will) the driving time from large land holdings to all of these urban phenomena—a necessary condition for marketing vacant land to consumers.

Every new community is bisected by, bordered by, or closely adjacent to a major freeway. Valencia (see Figure 3), for instance, is traversed by Interstate Route 5—formerly State Route 99. The road was made part of the state system in 1909. Contracts for constructing it to expressway standards were completed in 1949, and the route was declared a freeway in 1950. Kerry Patterson, Executive Vice President of the California Land Company, developers of Valencia, indicates that the presence of Route 99 as well as its completion as a freeway into

---

[1] For those freeways which are part of the Federal interstate system, the Federal government pays 90 per cent of the cost.

Los Angeles proper in 1963, proved to be one of the prime catalysts in the company's decision to develop.

The Irvine Ranch (area Y) was traversed by a major north-south road (Route 101) long before the decision by the Irvine people to proceed with University Community. Like 99, Route 101 became part of the State system in 1909. It was converted to a full freeway in 1958 and is now part of Interstate Route 5. Interchanges providing accessibility from 101 to the Ranch were designated in 1954—again long before the plans for the University Community at Irvine took shape. Three other major freeway routes linking Irvine with the rest of the Los Angeles metropolitan area were included for future construction in the 1959 California Freeway and Expressway System (Route 405, 55, and 73). Thus Irvine Ranch sits at a central point in the state's network of roads.

The development of Janss/Conejo fits the same pattern. The company's Vice President, Les Guthrie, states that "early in the game Janss engaged in a rather haphazard system of planning. While early plans were not premised on the state plan for highways, we soon realized the importance of Route 101 to their proposed development." As indicated earlier, 101 was taken into the state system by the State Highway Act of 1909.

Like Janss/Conejo and Irvine, Mission Viejo is linked with the entire metropolitan market by the San Diego Freeway, Route 101. There is one existing interchange on Route 101. This was designated at the time of conversion to freeway status in 1959.

North of the Los Angeles area, two new communities are in the process of development in the Sacramento area (see Figure 1). In both, the existence or proposed development by the state of a freeway produced expectations of growth and increasing land values.

Route 50, through the El Dorado Hills area, was adopted as a freeway in 1961, just before the initial sales campaign for El Dorado Hills. A freeway directly through the El Dorado Hills site is currently under construction.

Sunset City is bordered by Routes 65 and 80 northeast of Sacramento. Although the freeway alignment for Route 65

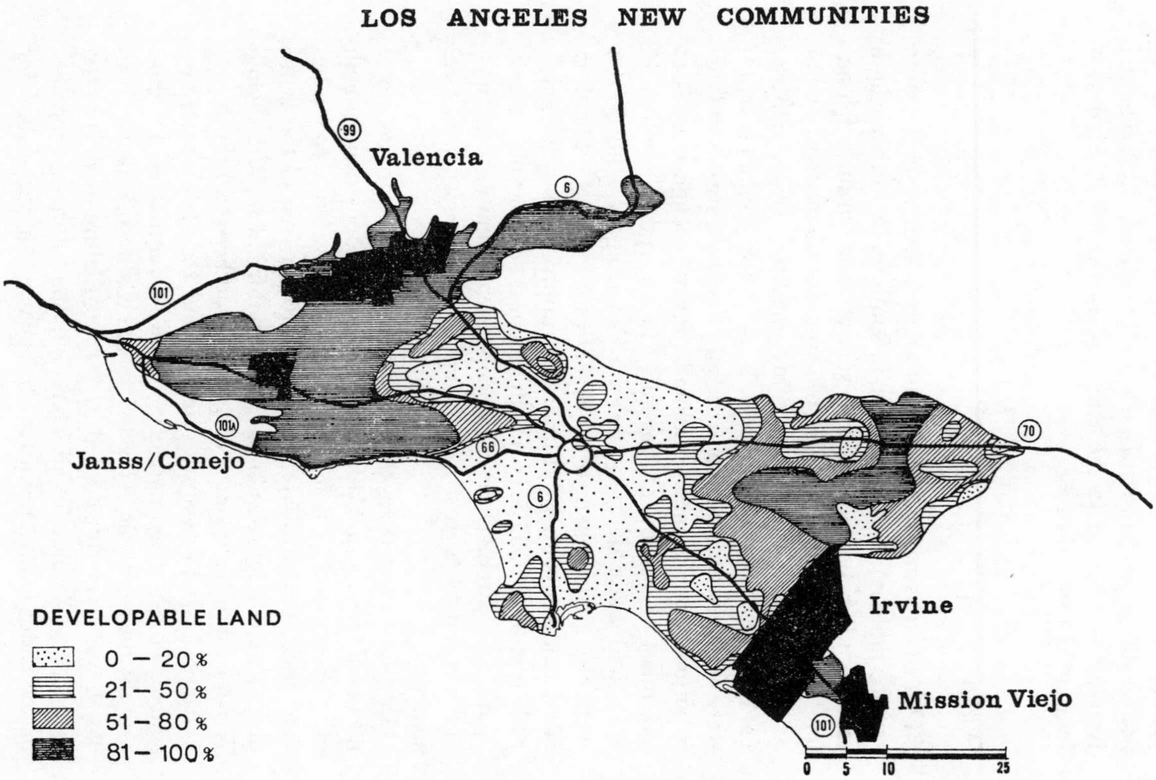
LOS ANGELES NEW COMMUNITIES
99
Valencia
6
101
101A
Janss/Conejo
66
6
70
Irvine
Mission Viejo
101
0
5
10
25
DEVELOPABLE LAND
0 — 20%
21 — 50%
51 — 80%
81 — 100%

FIGURE 3. Los Angeles new communities.

through the Sunset City site was adopted only in 1964 and will not be developed until 1972, Route 80 between Roseville and Newcastle—adjacent to the Sunset site—was constructed as a four-lane freeway in 1958.

Water

Given the unequal distribution of water resources in the state and the rapid rate of urbanization in Southern California, whose local supply is limited, the provision of water in that area has long been a problem. In 1928, to secure an adequate supply of water, 13 cities formed the Metropolitan Water District (MWD) of Southern California. In 1931, $220 million in bonds were authorized for the construction of a transmission and distribution system from the Colorado River, through more than 242 miles of aqueduct. Currently, 13 incorporated cities, 12 municipal water districts, and the San Diego County Water Authority are members of the MWD (see Figure 4). Members often contract with subdistricts to supply them with water. Although the MWD is by far the biggest supplier of water in Southern California, several independent county, municipal, and local districts exist also to supply local needs[2] from local sources.

Despite the success of the MWD in meeting the present water needs of Southern Caifornia, projected population growth makes it imperative that another source of water be found besides the Colorado River. More than 70 per cent of the water of California originates in the northern third of the state, while 77 per cent of the water need is in the southern two-thirds.

In 1947 the Legislature directed that the state's water resources be evaluated and that a plan be formulated for their orderly development. This led to the California Water Plan which was formerly adopted by the Legislature in 1959 as the recommended guide for all interests in the future development of the state's water resources. In essence the plan called for

---

[2] California has thirty-one General District Acts and many more Special District Acts.

LOS ANGELES STATE WATER PROJECT

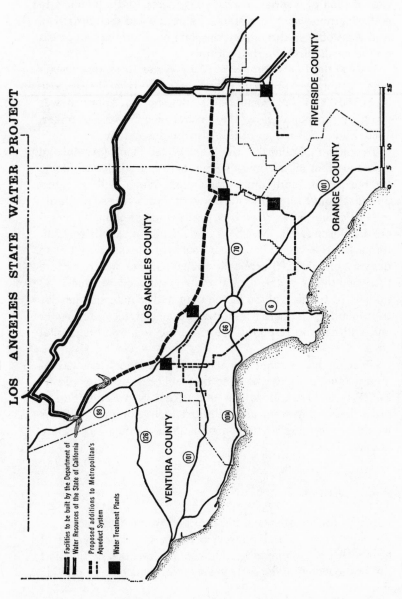

FIGURE 4. Los Angeles state water project.

the creation of a series of reservoirs, dams, and aqueducts to collect surplus water in northern California and then distribute it to areas of need throughout the state, with primary emphasis on the needs of southern California.

In 1959 the Legislature passed the Water Resources Development Bond Act (Burns-Porter Act), authorizing the issuance of $1,750,000,000 of general-obligation bonds. Approval was given by the populace in the general election of November, 1960. Figure 5 is a map of this distribution system.

To southern California, the State Water Plan represents an assurance that an adequate supply of water will be available for the present and future population. Water will be transported through aqueducts from northern sources, primarily upper Feather River reservoirs, to distribution points in southern California.[3] The Metro Water District of southern California has the largest single contract with the state (ultimate delivery of 1,500,000 acre feet annually), and will pay more than two-thirds of the capital costs (estimated to exceed $2 billion) of the first phase of the plan. Other independent districts serving southern California have contracted for water and will also be responsible for sharing some of the capital costs.

Given the heavy commitment of capital to launch a new community, guarantee by the state that sufficient water would be available to urban areas was one necessary pre-condition to make that outlay seem safe. Without such assurance, builders would be most unlikely to contemplate developing a new community.

Public Districts

Facilities for local sewage disposal and water distribution are the most costly initial improvements in the development of nearly all new communities. Only small fractions of this cost can be recovered in the early years of development. To provide

---

[3] Both northern and central areas in California will also receive water from the proposed system.

CALIFORNIA STATE WATER PROJECT

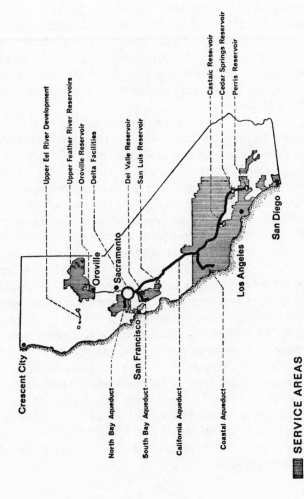

Upper Eel River Development
Upper Feather River Reservoirs
Oroville Reservoir
Delta Facilities
Del Valle Reservoir
San Luis Reservoir
Castaic Reservoir
Cedar Springs Reservoir
Perris Reservoir

Crescent City
Oroville
Sacramento
San Francisco
Los Angeles
San Diego

North Bay Aqueduct
South Bay Aqueduct
California Aqueduct
Coastal Aqueduct

SERVICE AREAS

FIGURE 5. California state water project.

such services to local users and to contract for it from a regional distributor such as MWD, it is necessary to have a legally qualified entity. Privately owned utility companies can be created for the purpose of distributing water, but without a known market for their services they find it difficult to raise capital under favorable terms. Of course, a developer-owner whose corporate and/or personal net worth is great enough can secure adequate financing, but then only by pledging his net worth as security. And even then financial institutions are frequently prevented by law and custom from making long-term loans for such purposes.

Since 1866, when the Legislature authorized the creation of water districts, the state has enacted general laws permitting as few as six residents to create a district to carry out one or more enumerated functions, among them the supply of water and the disposal of sewage. The districts are public authorities in that their governing board is elected (on a basis of assessed valuation) and they are permitted to issue tax-exempt bonds. The feature of tax-exemption and the fact that the district is a public agency, even though the only security for the bonds is the real property, makes the securities marketable under different terms and often to different investors than would be possible for a private utility. The effective interest rate often is less than 5 per cent, and principal payments are deferred in the early years. Most important of all, the repayment period can be thirty years or more. For all these reasons, then, the legal right to establish a new district has been a great aid in enabling developers to cut their initial costs and to realize their intent.

A district may be created not only under the general laws cited above but also by special act of the legislature; one example was the Estero Municipal Improvement District at Foster City. Details of this and other districts will be discussed in later chapters.

Conclusion

The general rise in incomes in the nation as a whole, and the supposed unrest with the quality of life in suburbia as outlined in the preceding chapters, suggested to certain developers the existence of a strong market for amenity-packed, planned communities. The events and legislative responses described in this chapter made it appear that in California this market was large, that sites were accessible, that water would be available, and that utilities could be financed. Indeed, without the assistance of state and local governments in California, most new communities now being developed would not have been initiated by their developers.

CHAPTER 4

The New Breed

The Californians

THE OPERATING style of a community builder is very different from that of a merchant builder. This stems almost entirely from the different goals each has set for himself. Both seek profits from real-estate development. But the merchant builder expects these profits from the rapid turnover of a product which he manufactures and merchandises to the consumers; the community builder's profits will come mainly in the latter stages of a long-range undertaking.

It is never easy to isolate real non-monetary objectives of business men from statements or actions which, calculated to improve their public relations, are intended mainly to help them meet financial goals. Entrepreneurs themselves are often unaware of the line which separates the two. Nevertheless, from interviews and conversations, it seems clear that community builders, reacting to the urban-development critique, have entered the field with a special sense of mission which few merchant builders hold. The latter essentially are committed to giving the consumer what he wants, which means a product similar to that which has recently been sold. The community builder, at least at the outset of his project, intends to be a leader in offering a product (here, a total environment) which has been heretofore unavailable. His assumption has been that prospective purchasers are eager to buy such a product and that many others can be educated to see its value and want it.

This section describes the nature of the community builder's intentions and the operational differences between him and the merchant builder, particularly in California. These differences

36

fall under the following headings: scale of project and time dimensions; methods of land assembly; use of city planners and other consultants; range of facilities; financial requirements; markets; and management structure.

INTENTIONS

As indicated, the urban-development critique sees comprehensive planning as a solution to the ostensible evils of laissez-faire urbanization. Appropriately, community builders describe their projects as places "with every consideration planned in advance in a complete new city," the converse being an "area where towns grow without plan."[1] There is great emphasis in the announcements of community builders on the variety and complete range of employment and recreation facilities to be included in the community. "We project a total community plan, which encompasses not only a careful balance of a variety of residential units and business and commercial facilities, but full provision for schools, churches, medical facilities, appropriate distribution of shopping areas, and last but not least, recreational facilities and country clubs."[2]

Both the financial and civic benefits of new communities were strengthened in their sponsors' eyes when a wave of laudatory articles appeared in national journals, including *Newsweek, Harpers, Time, Architectural Forum,* and the *New York Times.* Even the major trade magazine of homebuilding, *House and Home,* has praised the general intention of community building, as well as its profit potential, by calling El Dorado Hills "more than land planning on a vast scale . . . an attempt —backed by the profit motive—to offer homebuyers something better than the dreary sprawl that has marked explosive expansion around our cities."[3]

---

[1] El Dorado Hills Sales Brochure, 1964. Announced in 1958, El Dorado Hills, outside Sacramento, was the first new community.

[2] Morton Sterling, President of Sunset International Petroleum Company, in a speech to the Stanford Business School Alumni Association, March 18, 1964.

[3] *House and Home,* XXIII, 3 (March 1963), p. 106.

To make "total planning" effective, one must control a sufficient amount of land. The scale of such holdings and the resultant period of time it takes to develop them are of a very different order from the scale and time appropriate to the operations of a merchant builder. Aside from a very few exceptions (such as Lakewood in southern California, and the Levittowns), a large subdivider or merchant builder rarely works on a single parcel of more than 1,000 acres or 2,500 housing units. The largest merchant builders produce at most 700 to 1,000 housing units a year in any one location. A few may build a total of from 1,500 to 3,000 houses per year. Annual production of more than 200 houses (on about 70 acres) in any single location marks one as a large builder.

In comparison, the smallest new community, Foster City, contains 2,600 acres. Even this figure is misleadingly low because Foster City, near the heart of the San Francisco Bay Area, is planned for a higher density of units per acre than other new communities. Its plan calls for about 35,000 people to live in about 11,000 houses and apartments.

The largest new community holding is the 88,000-acre Irvine Ranch. Its owners, the Irvines, have made no public estimate of how many people will live on what is now their ranch, but it seems likely that the eventual population will be at least 250,000.

Irvine and Foster City are the extremes. Other holdings range as follows: the Newhall Ranch (Valencia) is 44,000 acres; Mission Viejo, 55,000 acres; Janss/Conejo, 10,000 acres; and Sunset Sacramento, 12,000 acres. With the exception of the Fosters, the builders of these and most other new communities project future population at over 100,000. If one were to pick a standard or typical number of acres and people, it would be 10,000 acres and 100,000 people. Some very large owners (Newhall and Mission Viejo) are making plans for part of their ranches to be developed at this scale.

Obviously, concern for, and investment in, a development of 10,000 acres or more must be thought of in terms of decades. Irvine will probably not be completed within the lifetime of anyone now working on it. Such an endless horizon has traditionally been anathema to the merchant builder.

PLANNERS AND OTHER CONSULTANTS

The relatively small scale on which the merchant builder works, and lack of commitment to design innovation as such, has meant that he generally by-passes the use of city-planning consultants or architects functioning as city planners. The intentions of prospective community builders and the size of their land holdings has made them much more receptive to such professionals.

As developers began to consider community building, they were informed by specialists in the field that the state of the planning art was equal to the task. Perhaps in such a social setting as a cocktail party, or at a conference on urban growth a Janss, an Irvine, or a Newhall met a city planning consultant or architect such as William Pereira, Victor Gruen, or Lee Ham,[4] who might have said: "You have the land and the money and you are a responsible citizen. My firm has or can assemble the skills in economic analysis, market research, engineering, and physical design to plan a whole city. Only in this way can you develop the land properly, and this means higher real estate values."

The involvement of such firms—Wilsey, Ham and Blair; Victor Gruen and Associates; and William Pereira and Associates—in city planning is a recent phenomenon, and their rise has been meteoric. Wilsey, Ham and Blair was a medium-sized civil engineering firm in 1955. By June, 1964 it had 220 employees, about a third of whom were engaged in city planning. Both Gruen and Pereira were, until recently, architects whose

---

[4] Wilsey, Ham and Blair were the planners of Foster City. Gruen has designed several communities, including El Dorado Hills, Valencia, and Laguna Niguel. Pereira did the original plan for Irvine.

only planning work was siting small groups of building like airports and shopping centers. Both offices now devote more than a third of their time to planning.

Perhaps the great stimulus to the involvement of many such firms in city planning was the enactment of the Federal 701 Program, part of the National Housing Act of 1954. Under this provision, the Urban Renewal Administration makes grants to cities and counties of up to two-thirds the total cost of the preparation of a general plan mapping out their future development. Rarely have cities or counties had the staff or inclination to do these plans themselves, and so they have turned to private consultants. Wilsey, Ham and Blair; Gruen; and Livingston and Blaney (a San Francisco firm planning new communities in Hawaii and San Jose) have all executed a great many of these general plans.

Convinced of the creative and technical ability of such firms, community builders similarly commissioned a general plan for all or a major portion of their sites. Sometimes they used such consultants as market analysts and economists, but their basic commitment was to the *designer*. Men like Gruen and Pereira, not economists or market analysts, were the leaders of the planning team. Their plan was prepared first and then subjected to review by other consultants who were clearly in a subordinate position, at least at the start. From a simple business point of view, such behavior on the part of community builders seems all the more remarkable when one considers that planning firms had had little or no experience in designing a market-oriented real-estate project.

Many early ideas of the designers were greeted with great enthusiasm by their employers. But as time wore on the plans came to seem less and less feasible, partly because costs estimates were high and partly because fears about consumer acceptance arose. Further, the disinclination of most community builders to undertake the effort (and the risk) to engage in detailed construction made significant portions of the plans unworkable. To date, plans for privately initiated new communities are little different from general plans adopted by many cities and counties in California. (A detailed record of the planning ideas proposed and rejected would make for a useful and interesting study.)

The subdivider or merchant builder is constantly searching for parcels of land that meet his varied requirements. Real-estate brokers bombard him with offerings of land which are or might be for sale. As indicated already, single purchases of over 1,000 acres are extremely rare.

Most merchant builders and subdividers seek land close to existing sources of employment as well as to shopping centers, schools, parks, etc. Larger builders prefer not to operate on less than 50 to 100 acres. Only then can they achieve both the rate of sale and economies of scale which are vital requirements for their financial success. In counties like Orange and Santa Clara, where much of the raw land is in fruit orchards, single holdings may be only 5 to 20 acres. The buyer trying to assemble enough of these small orchards to put together 100 or more contiguous acres frequently becomes a proper candidate for psychotherapy.

Farmers have become extremely sophisticated sellers. They are quite aware of their bargaining power when their 15 acres (on which the builder already has submitted offers) are absolutely necessary to make five other parcels, viable as a unit. Case studies of such dealings would make a fascinating story, but it is sufficient here to point out that land purchase—especially assembly of pieces of land held in separate ownership—is probably the most perplexing and important task of the subdivider or merchant builder.

Contrast this with the typical community builder: Most have owned the large ranches they are now developing for more than fifty years—Janss since 1911, Irvine since 1864, Mission Viejo (O'Neil Ranch) since 1906, the Newhall Ranch since 1875. Companies which are not developing family ranches, moreover, have almost without exception, purchased their land from a single owner. This is true for Foster City, Laguna Niguel, Rancho Bernardo, and Sunset Sacramento.

Community builders' problems, many of which we shall discuss, are myriad, but in California they do not have to scour the metropolis for 100 acres here or 200 acres there nor, worse yet, try to convince a recalcitrant owner that his 10 acres are really not worth $30,000 more than those of his neighbors.

Community builders, like subdividers and merchant builders, are in the business of turning raw land into housing sites. Large subdividers and merchant builders often have put in swimming clubs, golf courses, and parks to improve the marketability of their lots or houses. Some of them have developed neighborhood shopping centers to capture the increased value they have created by their own housing or lot sales. But there are two existing or proposed land uses for almost every new community which have rarely been a part of other operations: industrial parks, and regional shopping centers.

This is not to say that regional shopping centers and industrial parks do not exist close to the type of subdivisions built in the last two decades. In fact, if suburbia means large groups of housing developments with little or no major shopping facilities or employment centers, most of the development in California in the last 15 years should be given some other name. The major difference between the usual process and the new one is in who controls it. This difference, one of institutional form rather than physical result, will arise again in other contexts.

Until the advent of the community builder, the development of industrial parks and regional shopping centers was a specialized function. From time to time a merchant builder such as Bohannon, or Larwin engaged in such enterprises, but usually they were unrelated to his housing developments. (Hillsdale by Bohannon is an exception.) For example, Larwin Company is a large homebuilder, perhaps the largest in California. Yet while it specializes also in shopping centers, most of this activity is not related to its own housing projects.

Thus, in the rare instances in which merchant builders and subdividers do engage in regional shopping center and industrial park operations, they are then in a sense wearing different hats. But the community builder sees such operations as integral parts of his overall effort.

There has been much talk and writing about the absence of a full range of facilities in suburban California (as well as in other parts of the country), a void which some have said the community builders will fill. This is one of the themes of the urban-development critique. It may be due only to the fact that community building is still at an early stage, but we have been unable to find in the actual developments to date, or even in the plans for future developments, much that is not present in many California "unplanned" communities. Foster City has lagoons, and Janss has donated a little theater to Janss/Conejo; otherwise there is little else that is out of the ordinary.

The differences in facilities in subdivisions and in new communities may turn out to not be so much one of kind or quality but one of timing. It is likely that residents of new communities will get their parks, their golf course, their theater, their shopping center, their industrial park, and their schools slightly sooner and at higher levels of quality than their counterparts in regular suburban subdivisions.

POLITICAL RELATIONS

With minor exceptions, merchant builders and subdividers have been viewed with disfavor by county governments and even more so by city governments. These entrepreneurs have frequently fought zoning provisions, subdivision regulations, and building codes which tended to restrict their ability to market their product at the lowest price.

Such conflict need not be viewed as a matter of venality or irresponsibility. The fact is that government officials have one set of interests and developers another. Both sides usually make a considerable effort to accommodate to the other's point of view and frame of reference. Nevertheless their interests clash;

every merchant builder and subdivider commits a great deal of his time trying to ward off or reduce the restrictions placed upon him by local government.

For the community builder, the situation is markedly different. Some counties, such as Placer (Sunset/Sacramento) and El Dorado (El Dorado Hills), in confronting community builders have exhibited the traditional fears of a rural government suddenly faced with urbanization. Even here, however, the community builder ultimately is viewed with less alarm than are his traditional counterparts.

In the more urbanized counties—Orange (Mission Viejo, Irvine Ranch, and Laguna Niguel), Ventura (Janss/Conejo and the Albertson Ranch), San Mateo (Foster City), and Los Angeles (Ahmanson)—the community builder actually is seen by government as an asset. New planned-unit ordinances in several of these counties (Ventura and Orange), sponsored in part by specific community builders but applicable to other developments as well, have granted community builders almost all the freedom they want. We shall explore the reasons for such action in the chapter on political relations. Here, it is enough to note that it exists and to note how sharply it diverges from the situation facing merchant builders.

As already noted, the formation of new districts is a matter of special concern to community builders. In 1963, California had 4,799 special districts to carry out some governmental function—sewage disposal, water supply, park maintenance, street lighting, etc. These districts are governments, it will be recalled, because their directors are elected, because they can tax the property within their boundaries, and because they can issue tax-exempt bonds to make capital improvements. Many of them were created, in effect, by subdividers for two reasons. One was to establish some mechanism for the provision of services (street lighting, fire protection) which builders presumed customers would demand and which the county provided inadequately or not at all. The second was to acquire capital, otherwise unattainable or available only under prohibitive terms, through the creation of a public agency with bonding authority. It was assumed often that buyers would be less sensitive to costs paid in this manner (as taxes to a district) than to higher mortgage payments on a lot or a house.

The growing dominance of the merchant builder, less inclined than the subdivider to form districts, has reduced the number of districts newly created to finance basic site improvements or provide utilities. Also, an increasing percentage of new subdivisions are now situated within cities, which are already in the sewer and water business and which do not permit the formation of districts to finance on-site improvements.

For the community builder, however, the creation of a district has at times seemed necessary simply to launch his project. The legal and financial difficulties in providing sewage treatment and water supply for 10,000 or more acres not immediately adjacent to existing settlements are seen by many entrepreneurs in this field as their most critical hurdles.

At Irvine, the sewer and water districts that were formed issued $10.5 million in bonds. In 1960, El Dorado Hills wanted a similar district authorized in order to issue $50,000,000 in bonds. Janss owns both a private sewer company and water company to serve Janss/Conejo, but the community's water supply was still limited until the Los Angeles Metropolitan Water District brought a line to it. Indeed, from 1961 to 1964 Janss' rate of sale was hampered by shortage of water and delays in construction of sewage facilities.

Community builders are also very much concerned with changes in future political jurisdiction affecting their developments. Until recently, California law has made it very easy for only 500 residents to create a city, which then has the legal right to take over zoning control from the county. In other words, it would be quite possible for a new community to remove itself from the control and planning of its developer. The possible creation by new residents of a city government which might make major changes in the uses of the land rarely arises to worry the merchant builder. With his relatively small parcel of land, his time horizon also is much shorter. He frequently tries to secure changes from a city or county in zoning provisions, but his general concern with and attention to political relations, for the reasons outlined here, are far less dominant than they are in the operations of the community builder.

Although subdividers and merchant builders occasionally resort to the use of districts to finance off- and on-site improvements, this is not their usual method, nor are these the only areas for which they need financial support.

Traditionally, financial institutions (banks, insurance companies, savings and loan associations) have been limited by law and custom in making funds available for the purchase of land and the installation of site improvements. In the decade after World War II, merchant builders and subdividers often met their needs by ad-hoc syndication. (Whatever the method of financing, a land buyer always tried to get the seller to accept a small down payment and additional payment as lots or houses are sold.) Under this arrangement, they offered to friends handsome returns on money needed for the "front end" of a particular project. These amateur lenders were given a fixed time (usually one to two years) during which they would receive repayment of their investment as well as a percentage of the profits. The device attracted a variety of individuals with high incomes seeking profit which was taxable only at capital-gain rates. The different rates at which income can be taxed is discussed in Chapter 8. A few lost money, but rising land prices protected most investors, and netted high profit margins for many.[5]

For a variety of reasons, syndication lately has been on the wane. For one thing, savings and loan associations, as a part of

[5] Syndication was especially common in southern California where the industry's standing joke was that one's doctor would insist on discussing the next deal before diagnosing the ailment which had brought the patient to his office. In some jest we once offered to bet friends that the chances were better than even that one could find someone in a real-estate syndicate by ringing a door bell at random in Beverly Hills. Later all of us visited a screen-writer friend who, upon learning that one of us was in the home-building business, ran to his bedroom and returned with a map of 800 acres he and some colleagues were "interested in."

their rapid growth, now make funds available to merchant builders for land purchase and development. Also, some subdividers and merchant builders have operated at a profit long enough to use earned surplus and to borrow from a bank on a line of credit. Some banks have discovered that the laws are not so restrictive as they had once assumed, and that their traditional attitudes have cost them a potentially profitable source of loans.

Initial capital, however, is just one of several financial concerns of the merchant builder. With rare exceptions, he also gets a construction loan amounting to 75 to 80 per cent of the sales price of a house. This loan is to finance the structure and is to be repaid upon the sale of the house to the consumer. Such loans are somewhat risky, but highly profitable to the lender. The merchant builder is constantly searching for the best lender in terms of service, interest rate, fees, and the size of the loan. Even under the highly competitive conditions of the1960's, the combined interest and fees for constructing a $20,000 house (sales price) can run between $500 and $1,000.

The merchant builder sells directly to the consumer. Among methods of competing for the consumer's dollar is the attempt to offer him the most favorable financing terms. Sometimes this means FHA and VA loans which require complex, time-consuming dealings with Federal agencies; it always demands a never-ending search on the part of the builder for the lender who will make the highest loan, at the lowest interest rate, at a moment's notice, to any buyer, no matter what his income or credit rating.

Though financing is also very important to the community builder, his requirements and the character of his search are quite different. For one thing, the community builder does not construct houses for sale. (This will be discussed more fully below.) On occasion he sells lots to individuals, but in general he is not primarily in the business of offering a product directly to the consumer. Thus, he is relieved of the burden of negotiating for construction loans or permanent financing for owner occupants. He probably has come into contact with FHA for general approval of the development, but this is a routine matter. He does not deal with FHA or VA on specific subdivision approval, on valuation and specifications for houses, or on the credit qualifications of purchasers.

Those community builders who have owned land for fifty to one hundred years do not of course face the task of securing vast amounts of money to buy land. But community builders whose ancestors possessed less foresight must find sums of great magnitude (or convince the seller to accept a low down payment). The purchase price for land alone at Sunset/Sacramento was $14 million; at El Dorado Hills about $12 million; and at Foster City about $13 million. These are figures well beyond those paid by merchant builders for their considerably smaller tracts.

The earlier discussion of districts and political jurisdiction should have suggested that the community builder's acquisition of land or, if he has it already, his decision to develop is only the beginning of his financial problems. The initial or early outlay of funds—so that the first houses will be accessible to a freeway, will be hooked up to a decent sewage disposal system, and will have water—can be staggering. For Sunset/Sacramento, the costs were about $2.5 million, for Foster City over $10 million (mostly the cost of reclamation), for Janss/Conejo over $6 million. It is difficult to describe the precise financial exposure of a community builder at any given time, but it is evident that extremely large sums of money must be spent during the early stages of development before any sales can be made. It may be years or even decades before a sufficient rate of sale and development can be reached to service the interest on such capital, let alone repay the principal.

In addition to these mandatory capital outlays, there are discretionary commitments which community builders often feel compelled to make. Most build golf courses and club houses before there are enough people to support them; some install an elaborate network of landscaped roads not required to serve residents in the first year or two. These amenities are part of a marketing strategy to create a favorable image and to convince potential customers that the words and pictures in the brochures will shortly become a physical reality.

In brief, the merchant builder requires capital for two to five years for the purchase of land and the installation of site improvements. His methods of raising it include: syndication, short-term funds from savings and loan associations, short-term loans on corporate credit, and funds from earned surplus. Except for the last, the key characteristic of all these sources is "short-run." A community builder, on the other hand, usually requires not only about $10 million or more merely to initiate his development, but additional sums every year for five years or more unless other methods of long-term financing can be found. One such method is public districts; in the next chapter we shall describe another for a new community outside California.

THE MARKET

From time to time, subdivisions have been developed for middle and upper-income families in fairly remote locations. But the merchant builder "took over" in the late 1940's and, in the 1950's, went to fringe areas or beyond to lower his cost of land and site improvements and to get a large enough parcel to achieve economies in house construction. He assumed that most buyers would sacrifice proximity to work and more "established" areas for the better house value he could thus supply. The Levittowns, Lakewood, and other large developments are the best known manifestations of this process. Merchant builders who preferred to operate at a smaller scale and to cater to a different market looked for land closer in and paid higher prices to get it.

Community builders seem to be reversing the process. They are trying to sell in locations requiring longer journeys to work than developments created by merchant builders; yet the housing is by no means low priced.[6] For instance, the price range of the first houses in El Dorado Hills was $19,000 to

---

[6] In 1964–65 in California, a "low-priced" new house ranged from $12,000 to $16,000—which usually means, for buyers, annual incomes between $5,000 and $7,000.

$22,500. Later it rose to $22,000 to $25,000.[7] At Janss/Conejo it is $18,000 to $33,000; at Sunset/Sacramento, $23,000 to $38,000; at Laguna Niguel, $23,000 to $45,000 (with beach-front houses much higher); at Foster City, $23,000 to $45,000. It seems unlikely that in the early stages Irvine, Mission Viejo, or Valencia (all still being planned) will be different.

As a rule, then, few communities intend to offer houses at less than $20,000 during their first few years of marketing. This figure is not set entirely by costs or by the high land prices paid by merchant builders who construct the houses in new communities. It is the result of a conscious desire by community builders to create for their developments a certain kind of image, based on their perceptions of market behavior and future values. These perceptions will be analyzed in some detail in Chapter 6.

Every plan of a new community shows land earmarked and zoned for apartments. Many merchant builders don't build apartments at all. Those that do usually construct them on small sites separate from their single-family developments. Of the first 5,000 acres at Janss/Conejo (about half the total), 300 are zoned for apartments at a maximum density of 40 units per acre or a total of 12,000 units. No new community is far enough along to give any indication of the total volume of multi-family housing which it will contain. With the exception of one or two small apartment projects, none have even been started. The complex question of whether this is due to an absence of demand, land-pricing policies of the owners, or a calculated strategy to delay such development will be examined later. Whatever the reasons for the limited amount of apartment construction at present, community builders hope to incorporate multi-family housing on a significant scale.

As for the industrial parks included in every plan of a new community: of the 10,000 acres at Janss/Conejo, 1,000 are zoned for industry; at El Dorado Hills, 1,500 acres; at Foster

---

[7] The lower extreme has since fallen. By September, 1965, the price range began at $16,500.

City, 350 acres; at Irvine, 3,000 acres. It should be noted, however, that the mere designation of an area on a map or an acquisition of zoning does not immediately insure that there will be industrial takers for the space. At the moment, most new communities are still too young to have made any sales or leases to industry. Irvine and Janss have made some progress in this area. Irvine has three completed leases with 17 firms, including Ford, Collins Radio, and Douglas[8]—employing about 4,500 people. From 1960 to 1964, Janss attracted eight firms with 2700 employees. The few firms that have opened in new communities all fall into the category of light manufacturing or research and development. For many communities, a lack of rail facilities as well as limited utilities impede any effort to attract heavy industry. And, in California at least, there is a general surplus of industrial land. And even if customers representing heavy industry were available, it might well be that their presence would be considered harmful to the community image.

ORGANIZATIONAL FRAMEWORK

Some merchant builders and subdividers grew over a long period of time, adapting the operations of their firms to changes in demand and to other forces. These firms belong to families that have been in real-estate development and construction since the 1920's. Other builders, including some of the largest, entered the field only in response to the great, post-World War II opportunities.

Most merchant builders recognized at that time that the organization of building operations in general was woefully inefficient. As discussed in Chapter 2, the merchant builder did not then seek to make basic technological innovations. He began to systematize mass building through standardized design, specialization of labor, and more control over subcontractors. He tried, usually, to eliminate the distributor and

---

[8] Irvine Company estimates that by 1970 total employment by firms in its industrial park will reach about 15,000.

deal directly with manufacturers, to reduce unit costs, and to establish specifications simplifying on-site assembly.

Before World War II, lots or houses normally were sold by real-estate brokers, but most of the new merchant builders and subdividers, especially in California, now sell their product through their own personnel. They found that they could do this at a lower cost and far more effectively than could brokers, whom they regarded as having little or no competence in a mass market ruled by highly competitive conditions. Today, in addition to being their own salesman, these developers also manage their own merchandising directly; they landscape model homes, buy and install furnishings for models, write and design advertising, build signs, and so forth. On occasion, some of these functions are performed by outside contractors or agencies, but even then they are closely supervised and controlled by the merchant builder. It has been explained already that the problems of land assembly and financing are both important to and difficult for the merchant builder. Also he hires and supervises a civil-engineering firm to design the lot and utility layout. He hires a general contractor or a series of subcontractors to install the various components of site development—grading sewer lines, water lines, gas lines, streets, sidewalks.

The operations of the community builder may be as involved, or more so, but they are quite different in most respects. To date, it is possible to state categorically that no California community builder wishes to take on the task of constructing and selling houses to the general public for the profit inherent in that particular endeavor.[9] We shall discuss the reasons for this and other decisions in a later section, but it is enough to say here that, unlike the merchant builder, nearly every community builder is anxious to limit the size of his staff. This necessarily affects almost every decision about what he will do and how he will do it.

---

[9] The only exception to this statement is that some community builders are forced to construct houses when they can get no merchant builder to do the job they desire.

Merchant-building firms are generally owned and actively managed by one or two individuals. The larger companies have from five to ten second-line executives who are responsible for specific functions such as sales, advertising, purchasing, accounting, and construction. The principals concentrate on land purchase, financing, zoning, and product design.

In contrast, many community builders, especially historical land owners in California, are families with such substantial interests as oil production, banks, cattle breeding, income-producing real estate. Following the decision to launch a new community they have hired a project director, who is frequently the president or vice-president of a subsidiary corporation created for this purpose. For example, Charles Thomas, former Secretary of the Navy, is in charge of the development of the Irvine Ranch. Victor Palmieri, formerly with a large Los Angeles law firm, is President of the Janss Corporation (development arm of the Janss family). These managers tend to employ people with skills in political negotiation, law, engineering, and long-term experience in finance as opposed to the production and merchandising type of personnel sought by the merchant builder.

There are few examples of successful merchant builders, or other kinds of real estate firms, which have not been tightly controlled and directed by their owners. It remains to be seen if the community builders' delegation of authority to employee-managers will be as successful a mode of operation, in financial terms.

CONCLUSION

This section has focused on the many differences in style and operations between community builders and their predecessors (primarily merchant builders), in the California experience. As noted, these differences are the result of differences in scope and intent. The following section describes the planning stage for a new community in Maryland to show what happens when a developer has an especially strong sense of mission, and when the conditions of land ownership, politics, and economics are quite different from those in California.

Columbia, "A Garden for People"

On October 30, 1963, James W. Rouse announced his purchase of more than 14,000 acres of land between Washington, D. C., and Baltimore and his intention to turn the land into a new community. At first glance, the philosophical and physical background of Columbia seem identical to that of the new communities in California—the urban-development, critique, and rapid population growth. There were many significant dif-

LOCATION - COLUMBIA, MARYLAND

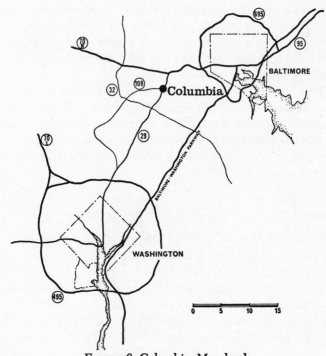

FIGURE 6. Columbia, Maryland.

ferences, however, in the conditions which Rouse faced and in the constraints he placed upon himself.

First, there are few large land-holdings between Baltimore and Washington, the area Rouse chose because of the rapid growth merging the two metropolitan markets (see Figure 6).

Second, although he is a successful business man, he does not possess inherited wealth as do many of the Californians.

Third, local government in Howard County, Maryland—the jurisdiction over Columbia—and in Maryland generally is structured very differently (and from the viewpoint of community builders, less helpfully) than in California.

Fourth, the State of Maryland had no laws permitting the creation of special districts, laws which in California do so much to ease the burden of financing sewer and water systems.

Fifth, Rouse, unlike the Californians, was willing to build an extensive operating staff and was anxious to explore the contribution of social scientists to the creation of a better environment.

This chapter, with emphasis on the above issues, describes the planning for Columbia. By July, 1965, the planning was nearly completed but actual construction was not expected to start until 1966. The story of Rouse's planning illustrates a basic tenet of this book—that community building is heavily influenced by economic, political, and physical realities, even though in the short run, a man whose zeal is especially strong may be able to bend these forces to his will.

THE MAN

James W. Rouse believes that there is a more-or-less direct relation between the quality of an environment and the quality of the people who experience it—that, in short, the better the environment, the better the person. In the broadest meaning of the term, then, good consequences are a matter of good design. The two men who head Columbia's planning team say: "We look to physical planning as the manifestation of social and aesthetic objectives."[10] In Rouse's own words: "Personally, I

---

[10] Morton Hoppenfeld and William Finley in a memo to James Rouse.

hold . . . that people grow best in small communities where
the institutions which are the dominant forces in their lives
are within the scale of their comprehension and within reach
of their sense of responsibility and capacity to manage."[11] It
is in terms of these general propositions—thus being put to a
test of validity—that Columbia is being built.

During the 1950's, Rouse (a founder of James W. Rouse
Company, one of the country's leading mortgage-banking
firms), was actively involved in many different public capacities with the state of the national environment. In the early
fifties, he was a member of President Eisenhower's Advisory
Committee on Housing, which produced many of the recommendations leading to the 1954 Housing Act. From 1958–1960
he was President and Chairman of the Board of Directors of
ACTION.[12] In 1961 he was Chairman of the subcommittee of
the Maryland State Commission which drafted the legislation
establishing the Regional Planning Council in the Baltimore
Metropolitan Area. He has also been a member of the Rockefeller Foundation's Advisory Committee on Urban Design,
and Chairman of the Greater Baltimore Committee. From these
experiences Rouse began to formulate certain ideas about the
way to meet the social, physical, and economic problems growing out of the country's increased and increasing urbanization.
By 1960 he had come to the view, strongly expressed in many
speeches and writings, that these problems were best attacked
through the combined means of renewing the central cities
and developing new communities in suburban or exurban
areas. Such new communities, he thought, should be small
enough to permit personal control and participation but large
enough so that little or no financial aid from the state or Federal
government would be required. He believed that a city of
100,000 to 125,000 people was the ideal size.

In 1957, Rouse was instrumental in forming the Community
Research and Development Corporation (hereafter called

---

[11] From an interview with Rouse, April, 1964.
[12] Action Committee to Save Our Neighborhoods.

CRD), whose aim was to buy, develop, and manage real-estate properties.[13] An unusual aspect of CRD is that it emphasized management as well as development; most such companies sell their properties after developing them. The birth and development of Columbia is part of the history of CRD.[14]

FINANCING

The idea to build a new community had been in Rouse's mind for several years when, in the summer of 1962, he had the CRD Research Department prepare a prospectus (called the "green book") to convince the corporation's board members that such a large-scale project was economically feasible. Rouse kept looking for sites in the Washington and Baltimore Metropolitan areas where a community might be developed. But the land that was to serve as the site of Columbia came into the possession of CRD largely as a result of chance.

In May, 1962, one of the corporation's board members learned that 1,000 contiguous acres were available for purchase in Maryland's Howard County. Since expectations were that Howard County would more than double its 1960 population, and since CRD wanted to diversify its interests, the corporation decided to buy the land. It would provide a good site if CRD wanted to build tract houses or a large subdivision; if the corporation decided not to move in this direction, the land could be sold in a few years for a capital gain.

CRD contracted to buy the acreage on the basis of a 180-day settlement date. The purchase price was just over $600,000, almost $200,000 of it to be paid in cash at the time of settlement. Just prior to settlement, in September, 1962, a smaller parcel of land (428 acres) adjoining the 1,000 acre tract be-

---

[13] Rouse Company owns 30 per cent of CRD's stock and, on a contract basis, both manages CRD and provides it with its staff.

[14] At the time of this writing (September, 1965), CRD has concentrated on the development and management of enclosed-mall shopping centers. Construction of the company's first residential community, the Village of Cross Keys, was begun in September, 1963 on a 68-acre tract in Baltimore.

came available, and the corporation purchased it on the basis of a 90-day settlement date. The cost was $400,000, $105,000 in cash and the balance payable in ten years.

With the acquisition of this new parcel of land, it became evident to CRD that if it chose to do so, it could acquire sufficient acreage to put together either a very large aggregation of subdivisions or a new community.

The corporation now had approximately 1,500 acres, for which it had invested almost $300,000 in cash and obligated itself for another $700,000. But these were miniscule expenditures in terms of the outlay that a new community would demand. As a result, the corporation decided to continue purchasing such land as was available, but did not fully commit itself to building a new community. Nevertheless, there was enthusiasm about the basic market potential of the site. Not only were the Baltimore and Washington areas growing rapidly, but they were growing together in such a way that land in the five corridor counties, of which Howard was one, might draw consumers from both metropoli. From 1940 to 1960 the population in these counties increased by 245.6 per cent. It was expected to rise by another 95.7 per cent by 1980. Figure 4 shows the relationship of Columbia to Washington and Baltimore.

Once CRD made the decision to continue purchasing land, it became apparent that it would need a new source of capital to meet settlement dates and mortgage payments on earlier acquisitions and to provide funds for overhead and further land acquisition. The aim was to secure sufficient funds at reasonable interest costs with sufficient time for repayment. Also, the interim financial arrangements for land acquisition would have to be structured so as not to prejudice corporate efforts to secure later development funds.

Rouse's first attempt to secure capital received a neutral reception. Then after some preliminary informal contact, Rouse in December, 1962, wrote to an "old friend," the Connecticut General Life Insurance Co., which for a good number of years had been a source of funds for many of his successful commercial developments. Rouse outlined the needs of CRD and suggested the creation of a new development corporation which would be a fully owned subsidiary of CRD. The investor would advance funds to the corporation for land acquisition. Security would consist of debentures or preferred stock issued by the development corporation, and the corporation would pay the investor a 10 per cent increase in the value of the stock for each year that the debt was outstanding. In addition, the lender would be granted an option to participate further in the development. In the event that stock was not redeemed within ten years, the holder would have an option to acquire all the common stock and achieve full ownership.

Rouse believed that sufficient land for a development could be acquired within 18 months, and he estimated that the contract price for 12,000 acres would be $18 million with $6 million expended in cash. His proposal also included details on how specific purchases would be handled.

On the basis of this outline, CRD and Connecticut General entered into protracted negotiations. They reached a tentative settlement in March, 1963—when the insurance company provided CRD with an interim loan of $2 million (soon increased to $3 million)—and reached a more or less permanent arrangement in May, when Connecticut General agreed to lend CRD a total of $18 million. (This figure was increased to $21 million by October, and later to $23 million.) CRD was to draw such monies from this sum as it needed for land acquisition. Collateral took the form of 8 per cent first-deed trust notes due April 30, 1967. CRD committed itself not to exceed an average acreage cost of $1500. Accumulative simple interest (no compounding) and principal payments would be due upon settlement.

From the outset of the negotiations, it was clear that the insurance company intended to become more than an investor in the new corporate structure to be created on the basis of its loans. In the final settlement, Connecticut General received the right to select three out of the five members of the new firm's board of directors. CRD would select the other two. All 2,000 shares of stock would be held by Connecticut General.[15] Thus the new firm—the Howard Research and Development

---

[15] One thousand shares of Class A stock, at $1.00 value, were owned outright; the remaining 1,000 shares of Class B stock, also at $1.00 value, were owned by CRD but pledged to Connecticut General.

Corporation, to which Rouse was elected as president—emerged as an affiliate rather than a subsidiary of CRD.

CRD agreed to manage the new firm on a fee basis, with payments deferred until development. Although not a matter of formal agreement, there was an understanding between CRD and Connecticut General that the insurance company would have an option to participate in the development in some capacity after the land acquisition phase. Before the settlement date on the deed of trust notes, CRD was required to present the company with a completed plan and financial program. Expectations were that the deeds of trust due in 1967 would be refinanced at 6 per cent (10-year notes) with accrued interest added on to the principal obligation.

To date almost the entire $23 million loan has been encumbered by land acquisition, with approximately $18 million utilized in cash and $6 million committed in purchase-money mortgages. Because the loan has been used to "take out" any of CRD's equity in land, the corporation's only cash outlay to date has been approximately $750,000 for planning.

SECURING THE LAND

Early in 1963, with capital potentially secured and with an immediate loan of $2 million in hand, CRD decided to go ahead with plans to build a new community. It had two alternatives for methods of acquiring the necessary land: to procure contiguous properties, acquiring one property at a time; or, literally, to buy all over the place. Under the "shot-gun" approach, it was probable that CRD could acquire more properties in a shorter period of time. Yet Rouse feared that he might end up with a land pattern resembling a piece of Swiss cheese. On the other hand, although the incremental approach potentially promised a coherent package, it contained the dangerous risk of revealing CRD's intentions and thus placing the firm in a disadvantageous bargaining position.

After much debate CRD decided to purchase land within the general target area wherever and whenever it became available—a somewhat modified "shot-gun" approach. It would make no attempt to secure all the large properties at once. It based its acquisition plans on an 18-month time period.

The story of Rouse's negotiations with land owners over the next months reads like a James Bond novel; secret rooms, plot strategy, and dummy corporations characterized the process. To reduce the possibility that land owners would become aware of CRD's intention to build a community, Rouse created shell corporations under such names as Serenity Acres, Cedar Farms, and Potomac Estates. Each of the corporations contracted with a different realtor. Their "separate" activities made it appear that there were several unrelated efforts in the area to establish a number of small-scale subdivisions.

All this behind-the-scenes sleight-of-hand reveals the difficulties of acquiring a large site when ownership is distributed among hundreds of individuals. Moreover, because of its agreement with Connecticut General, CRD was committed to spending no more than an average of $1,500 per acre. In the six-month period between April and October, Rouse dealt with 328 individual owners and made over 140 separate purchases. Strategy was determined on a day by day basis in terms of each piece of property, the personality of the owner, and his financial position. At the end of the six-months period, surprising even itself, CRD was able to announce that its affiliate, the Howard Research and Development Corporation, had secured slightly less than 15,000 acres midway between Baltimore and Washington. Average cost per acre was $1,450.[16]

There remained—and still do to this date—five "holdouts," totalling 850 acres.

COLLEAGUES AND THE WORK GROUP

It is difficult to document neatly the depth of Rouse's belief in the importance of a community as a potential determinant

---

[16] CRD worked out a variety of arrangements with the larger land owners. It granted life estates—especially to aged individuals—and once it allowed an owner to retain fee-simple titles to small portions of his land. Deferred settlements, options to buy, cash deals, and long-term leases were some of the many methods employed by Rouse, separately or in combination, to acquire varying rights in the land.

of people's happiness. He is a deeply religious man, not in the sense of devotion to the practices and beliefs of one organized group but in his devotion to the so-called Protestant ethic. He thinks most American clergymen spend too much time constructing buildings and organizing and not enough time working with people. For his part, though he works very hard, because of his highly individual notion of the needs of a good life, Rouse rarely schedules a meeting on a week-end or interrupts a vacation to respond to a business emergency. In conversation he has used the term "God-centered" to characterize what he hopes Columbia will be.

Rouse is a self-made man. It is part of his ethic that Columbia will have less meaning for him *and* for society if it is not a financial success. Rouse made his position clear in an interview.

I am socially responsible, not socially self-conscious. There is no incompatibility between making a profit on substantially a very risky endeavor with a large capital outlay and achieving a community which provides the highest environment for the growth of people. . . . The profit motive disciplines any goal structure. Every goal is strengthened and made valid by contributing to make a profit. People will pay for a better life. . . . If our efforts are to be copied by other private institutions, we must show a large profit.

Rouse believes people have great capacity to grow, to do better if given a chance. After his initial efforts at land acquisition and financing, Rouse in effect gave that chance to the two men he asked to join him in directing the planning of Columbia.

In the fall of 1962, Rouse hired William Finley as project director of Columbia. Finley, an experienced administrator and negotiator, received the first Bachelor's and Master's degrees given by the Department of City Planning at the University of California in 1949. Until the opportunity at Columbia, his entire career had been in work for local government—first in Richmond, California, where he was Planning Director, and later in Washington, D. C., where he was the Director of the National Capital Planning Commission. In the spring of 1963, Finley hired Morton Hoppenfeld as chief designer for Columbia. Hoppenfeld also had received his Master's degree in City Planning at Berkeley and, like Finley, had worked entirely for

public agencies. He had been Chief of Special Area Planning
for the Philadelphia Planning Commission, and later had
worked under Finley as Urban Designer for the Capital Planning Commission. Hoppenfeld, with undergraduate training
in architecture, is a physical designer. Both these men brought
with them a commitment to public service—to the general
welfare—as well as valuable understanding of the workings of
local government. Both came to Columbia hoping that Rouse's
resources, ability, and objectives would offer them a major
opportunity to put their own skills to work on a great undertaking.

Soon after arriving, Hoppenfeld, interested less in the esthetics of design than in its relation to behavior, suggested that
CRD bring together a group of individuals trained in various
relevant disciplines, (mostly the social sciences) to function
as an extended arm of the planning staff. The "work group,"
as it soon became known, hopefully would provide the staff
with firmer insights into the social needs of the new community
and with a clearer sense of the social objectives for which it
should aim. The whole effort would be a unique attempt to
unite social and physical planning.

During the summer and fall of 1963, Rouse, Finley, and
Hoppenfeld formed a 14-member work group whose participants ranged among many occupations and academic disciplines, from city managers to education specialists, economists
to professors of psychology.[17] Donald Michael, social psycholo-

[17] The committee members were: Henry Bain, Jr. consultant in Public
Administration and Business; Antonia Handler Chayes, Technical Secretary
to the Committee on Education, President's Commission on Women;
Robert Crawford, Commissioner of Recreation for Philadelphia; Dr.
Leonard Duhl, psychiatrist at the National Institute of Mental Health;
Nelson Foote, sociologist and Manager of Consumer and Public Relations
Research Program, General Electric Company; Herbert Gans, Professor
of Sociology at Columbia; Robert M. Gladstone, President Robert Glad-
stone and Associates, economic research and market analysis; Christopher
Jencks, education specialist and education editor of the *New Republic*;
Dr. Paul Lemkau, Professor of Public Health and Psychiatry at Johns
Hopkins; Donald Michael, chairman; Chester Rapkin, Professor of City
Planning, University of Pennsylvania; Wayne Thompson, City Manager
of Oakland, California; Alan Voorhees, Transportation Consultant; and
Stephen B. Withey, Professor of Psychology, University of Michigan.

gist and resident fellow at the Institute for Policy Studies, Washington, D. C., was appointed chairman.

Before the first meeting of the work group, Hoppenfeld sent its members a memo outlining their task as he saw it.

> In suggesting what we can do, let us be clear that the goals for this project are not utopian; we want to apply the social sciences to the actual design and operation of a new community better than it has been done before. . . .
>
> In essence, what should come out of our efforts is a better basis for making specific decisions about the social design of the community. . . .
>
> For you particularly it will demonstrate the applicability of the behavioral sciences under actual operating conditions.

He closed these remarks with a firm demurrer:

> But, precise or vague as your recommendations are, the final decision necessarily will be ours, the developers, as to whether or not to use them and to what extent.

The work group, Rouse, and his staff, held their first meeting in the fall of 1963. At first, the atmosphere was pervaded by a sense of skepticism. The work-group members were dubious about "state of the arts"—that is, over specifically how much they would be able to help the Columbia project. In response to this feeling, both Rouse and Finley spoke, assuring the group of their own deep interest and the values they felt surely would result from its deliberations.

The group decided to devote its future meetings to the presentation of papers by individual members, concerning the particular area of community life or development (education, recreation, etc.) which fell within the purview of their expertise. The papers were to outline the alternative methods of approach open to a new community. From these alternatives, chairman Michael, and two committee members, Henry Bain, Jr., a consultant in public administration, and Robert M. Gladstone, an economist and market analyst (who together constituted Rouse's inner "brain trust" in conjunction with Rouse and his staff, would select one alternative for each specialist to explain in detail. Bain would bring to bear his knowledge of Maryland's political and institutional forces, and Gladstone his economist's knowledge of the market. Each of the second presentations was to include statements of: 1) the objectives for the community in the particular area under analysis; 2) the level of services to be provided; 3) the physical facilities needed; 4) the appropriate financing techniques; and 5) the critical lines of interaction between the area under analysis and other aspects of the community. After a critique of each presentation by other members of the work group and by Rouse's staff, Michael would be author of an integrated document.

In developing their initial proposals, members of the work group were told to ignore economic, political, or market considerations that might serve as constraints. They were to think boldly and imaginatively, their only point of reference being the very loose framework of community goals articulated by Rouse at the opening of the session.

Between November, 1963 and February, 1964, the work group met five times. Each meeting generally lasted two days and was oriented around specific presentations by individual members. A final work group meeting was held in August, 1964. At this time Michael presented his integrated study for review, and the physical plan of Columbia was "unveiled" to the group for critique.

THE CONCERNS OF THE WORK GROUP

The deliberations of the work group clustered around three concerns: 1) the political relationship between the residents of the community, and between the residents and the developer; 2) the methods for establishing channels of communication both within the community (among the residents, and between them and the developer) and out from the community to the local areas and people surrounding it; and 3) the relations between physical and social planning.

Does the concept of a new community imply a new definition of the role of local community government? How can the desire of the developer to control the development at least during its initial years be equated with his hope that the community will foster self-government as well as extensive intra-group and individual participation? What influence should early residents have on the long-range development of the community? These questions filled many hours of discussion in the work group.

Several members (notably Henry Bain) approached the questions by redefining the traditional concept of government as such. Rather than to treat government as a single structural entity, the group posited that "government" in a new community would consist of many different entities, some private, some public, some quasi-public. Each of the entities would be responsible for carrying out or achieving different community programs, each would find its own appropriate balance on community and developer participation, and together their collective action would constitute the community's government.[18]

The second main concern of the work group was communication and how to increase effective communication both within the community and between the residents and outside areas. The group proposed that several varieties of "conveyor belts" be incorporated in the community design to provide for easy transmission of ideas, goals, services, and finally people. The recommendations dealt with the "belts" themselves—that is, the roads, pathways, airways, and so forth—and the "collecting nodes"—that is, the geographic locations where people, goods, and information gather and are gathered.

For example, the group thought that internal circulation between villages and to the town center would be facilitated by a mini-bus system operating on its own right of way. Such a method of transportation would reduce the need for a second car and increase female, teenage, and aged mobility—and also would help promote the community's image. The group further

---

[18] The group came to this redefinition by an analysis of a government's functions. It saw three of them: 1) regulating human behavior (including the behavior of organizations); 2) allocating resources; and 3) performing services. Further, a government performed the three functions in four not necessarily exclusive ways: 1) through sovereignty; 2) through deed restrictions or covenants; 3) through the market; and 4) through belief. Given this analysis, it was a relatively short step to the idea of a plurality of entities performing the different functions of government in a variety of ways.

suggested that a liberal sprinkling of foot and bridle paths be provided throughout the community, as well as space for neighborhood meetings, local message centers, and a community television station. Perhaps the most interesting proposal concerned a modern renovation of the old "Mom and Pop" village store. The work group proposed that such stores be established in each neighborhood, owned and operated by a community-wide nonprofit organization. The stores would combine entrepreneurial with administrative and social functions. They would provide daily needs in certain standard commodities such as food and medicines; serve as a combination restaurant-meeting hall; distribute information about community affairs; act as a checkout and storage facility for recreation equipment in lower-income neighborhoods; and assist in the management of neighborhood social centers. The work group thought it likely that the stores would have to be subsidized (by the residents or the developer) with funds secured from other activities.

For any of these proposals concerning communication processes to succeed (and for Rouse to market the community), most members of the work group felt Columbia should maintain a homogeneity among its residents at the block and small neighborhood level.

The community as a whole should include all kinds of people in all kinds of desirable housing and environments. The community as a whole should encourage social interchange and communication in politics, recreation and leisure time activities. In blocks and small neighborhoods, however, social homogeneity is desirable to avoid friction and the kind of keeping-up-with-the-Jones that can cause both the Smiths and the Joneses to go broke.

While in a sense the whole community was to be an education in living, the work group also proposed several recommendations specifically oriented towards Columbia's educational program. It advised that team teaching and ungraded classes be introduced at the elementary school level, and that arbitrary divisions of primary education be dropped in favor of elementary schools of whatever size the neighborhood population required. Education should be provided through the twelfth grade—in a combination either of two years of junior high and four years of high school, or four years of middle school and then four of high school. Meeting rooms, recreational facilities, and libraries in the schools should be designated for public as well as student use, thereby providing a wide range of educational and recreational opportunities to all community residents.

Rouse, and several members of the work group, believed that Columbia should aim for small schools as focal points of small villages. The group proposed that elementary schools, of kindergarten through the fourth grade (initially to be housed in unsold, unused housing units), were "the most appropriate physical scale for youngsters." The villages were to be planned to contain no more than a thousand students of high-school age. The group felt that small schools would increase personal participation among the students, while closed-circuit television and inexpensive bus service would provide the variety found in larger schools. Finally, the group suggested that the entire educational program at Columbia be treated as an "experiment" and become part of the research-and-development program of one or more of the major colleges in the area.

Other work-group recommendations related to the general health of the community as well as to the health of its individual members. "The accent should be on prevention and early diagnosis." Suggestions were put forth for both individual and group medical practice, while a comprehensive health-insurance plan was proposed for all residents. An Institute of Human Development was also discussed by the work group, who conceived of it as having four objectives: 1) to provide for adult and family education; 2) to provide supplementary education for children; 3) to develop innovative educational techniques; and 4) to study the problems and opportunities created by increased leisure time and automation.

Since the planning for Columbia is still going on, and since many of the recommendations or ideas of the work group may be implemented at later stages of development, the group's full contribution cannot be assessed at this time with great certainty. The school district has reduced its elementary school size from 750 to 550 students. Howard County has only one school district, which mitigates against a special program for Columbia. On the other hand, the mini-bus system has been made an integral part of the plan with provisions for a special right-of-way for this purpose which locates higher-density housing along the route. The modern version of the Mom and Pop store has been adopted. There is now no way to tell if such ideas as community-wide health insurance and the special governmental arrangements will become reality.

In summary, it appears that Rouse and his staff did not get any real breakthroughs from the work group in planning for a new community. But this failure, it should be stated, results chiefly from the difficulty of innovation in this area[19] and is not a reflection of the abilities of the work group.

ECONOMICS AND COLUMBIA

As explained, the "green book" was drafted in 1962 as a brief analysis to show what monetary returns might be expected from building a new community. When Rouse hired the economist Robert Gladstone, his first tasks were to participate in the work group, and to refine the cash-flow projections of the green book for use in securing capital.

Gladstone realized immediately that "refinement" of the green book entailed major market studies and close liaison with the planners. He pointed out that both sale rates and costs could vary widely depending upon the type of plan devised. It was noted in the first section of this chapter that when the Californians used economists or market analysts, they were hired to prepare "one-shot" studies based on a finished plan. In Columbia, the situation was quite different. Gladstone became virtually a member of the staff. He was to provide almost daily judgments about local market conditions and the likely relation between the cost of a planning proposal and the potential market response. In addition, he was to devise an

---

[19] For a detailed discussion of this factor see Herbert Gans' forthcoming study, *The Levittowners*.

accounting system that would clarify the relation between cash flow and the return on capital.

The green book had presented to its readers (the CRD Board and their potential equity partners) a very positive cash-flow picture for a potential new community in the area of possible major land acquisition. Twelve thousand acres between Baltimore and Washington purchased at an average cost of $1,500 each within a three-year period was the assumed target. Approximately 30,000 units were projected for 100,000 people. The sale of land over the development period, and the leasing and sale of industrial and commercial land would result in a profit of $67 million.

Gladstone's revisions of the green book in November, 1963, approximately a year and a half after the original presentation, confirmed the early optimism and gave a renewed impetus to the whole endeavor.[20] When, however, tentative sketch plans began to be refined during the winter of 1964 and the consultants dealing with infrastructure (water, sewer, major roads, parks, etc.) brought in their preliminary cost estimates, projected profits were much lower. The process was both enlightening and painful to all the participants. Finally in June, 1964, Gladstone submitted Working Paper 16 which was both a model accounting system and an updated cash-flow analysis.

According to Working Paper 16, 25,600 units would be developed over a more realistic 15-year period (more realistic than the 12-year period in the original green book) on the entire 14,035 acres then under Rouse's ownership. Charges for water distribution and sewage disposal by the Howard County Metropolitan Commission were minimized by assuming a negotiated cost of development, and a connection fee based on

---

[20] The first papers prepared by Gladstone assumed a population of 150,000 (17 per cent of the entire projection for the corridor) and a unit count of 44,000. Working Paper 5 (November 1963) used the same assumptions relative to density, land prices, and land allocation as did the original green book. It was therefore not a true test of the green book. The number of units in this revision was increased to 32,000 (green book, 30,000) and the population to 112,000. Development would be on 14,000 acres rather than the earlier 12,000. In Working Paper 8 the number of units projected increased to 37,000 and the population to 120,000. The development was scheduled for ten years with an average unit production of 3,700 a year.

the charges found in a contiguous county ($650 per house and $100 per apartment). A third-year lag (caused, in part, by the early minimal assessment base) in county repayment of school costs was posited, revealing that Rouse would have to expend heavy outlays for initial school funding. Almost 8,000 units (including 2,000 apartment units) were programmed during the initial five-year development period, and 80 per cent of the land was to be sold as finished lots with an over-all single-family density of 3.5.

Working Paper 16 reflected a detailed attempt to coordinate economic analyses with the new community's emerging plan. Prior to this time, the planners could add very little to the green book assumptions and the loose analysis prepared on its basis by Gladstone. From 16 came a more sober picture of net developer involvement and eventual profit.

It revealed that the net profit of an investment of over $100 million, in an extended development period of fifteen years, would be less than $10 million.

Rouse and company were not pleased. As he expressed it, to make this endeavor work, "we must double our money every five years." Where was the money to come from? With a strong mandate from Rouse, the planners and economists looked to reducing the number of acres in open space, increasing density, speeding up the development pace, reducing developer involvement through the special-district approach, and reevaluating the acreage devoted to industry.

A decision, primarily based on political considerations, was made to plan only for the contiguous property owned by Rouse. This reduced the total land under planning from 15,000 to approximately 11,700 acres. More than 1,000 acres were shifted from open space to residential and commercial use. This, along with changes to higher densities, increased the number of housing units from 25,600 to 27,700.

When Gladstone recommended switching land use from open space to residential or industrial, he was asserting, in effect, that any marketing value accruing from leaving land open would be more than offset by the revenues which would be derived from other uses. He was, of course, dealing here only with monetary issues, not with any loss to the general or societal interest because of the plan change. Gladstone's judgment was accepted and is almost certainly sound.

It is, however, not so apparent that plan changes can *increase* the *rate of sale* (or lease) of land—the absorption rate. In January, 1964, prior to preparation of Working Paper 16, an estimated average development rate of 3,700 units per peak year was projected. However, Gladstone determined that this rate was probably unattainable and used 2,500 per year instead in Working Paper 16. Rates of absorption for commercial and industrial land were assumed to be directly related to residential growth. When Working Paper 16 showed a low profit margin, the conversions from open space were made, but it seems there were also changes in assumed rates of sale. We do not understand why this would be so—that is, if the market determinations in Working Paper 16 were reasonable, wouldn't the reduced amenity (less open space) decrease the sale rate? We shall discuss this analytical method and its implications in more detail in Chapter 9.

As of July 1, 1965, Columbia planned to offer in the first two years houses priced from $18,000 to $45,000, garden apartments with monthly rentals from $120 to $175, and town houses selling from $22,000 to $28,000. No lower priced housing is to be offered until market experience has been gained. The table gives the projected volume for this two year period.

Single family detached	
$18,000–23,000	600 units
24,000–28,000	250
30,000–35,000	100
35,000–45,000	50
	1,000
Single family detached total	1,000
Golf course lots	200
Apartments	200
Town houses on Lake 1	50
Total	1,450

Gladstone's analysis of the strengths and weaknesses of Columbia is based on a point of view similar to that of the Californians. The advantages he sees are the facilities, the developer's control over the builders, and, if necessary, favorable financing terms given to builders on land sales. In another sense, the latter is also a disadvantage because it raises costs. In addition, there is the disadvantage of Columbia's distance from its surrounding metropolitan areas. Assessing all this, Gladstone maintained, as of July, 1965, that from 1970 an average annual absorption rate of 2,500 housing units could be achieved.

Two aspects of Columbia's present plan and marketing strategy—each of which will help determine the time at which money must be spent, or will be received, and thus have a significant effect on profits—should be noted. The first is the plan's mix of type of units and density per village. The plan calls for considerable difference among the villages. For instance, Village One, the first to be erected, will contain little or no low-density development. Therefore, for Columbia to offer a variety of housing types from the outset, it will have to build roads, utilities, and the like in several different places. In this way, the development will have to spend more funds earlier than if its marketing were confined to a compact area.

The second aspect of Columbia's strategy which will affect its profits is the financial terms HRD intends to give to builders who purchase land from it and also the level of improvements HRD intends to install. On the one hand, if Rouse permits builders time to pay for the land, they will be more likely to build in Columbia.[21] On the other hand, such a policy creates financing problems for Rouse. Again, if he decides to sell in the form of finished lots (with interior roads and utilities completed), he will have to accept an additional financial burden —in terms of the gap between his payment for the site improvements and his receipts from the builder. At present, the decision is to sell about half the lots for medium density housing as

---

[21] At times builders can get such financing from sources other than the land owner.

finished and the other half in bulk to large merchant builders. All of the low- and high-density sites are to be sold finished.

POLITICAL RELATIONS

In general, Rouse wanted the same things from local government as did the Californians: 1) zoning which would permit maximum freedom to offer the highest densities the market would absorb and would guarantee his right to capitalize on the commercial and industrial demand; 2) authority to create an entity which could issue tax-exempt bonds; 3) legislative guarantees that such zoning and district provisions would be under his control for most of the development period (and not be shifted "prematurely" to the residents) and 4) assurance that roads and utilities would be brought to his site at reasonable cost.

The political setting he encountered, however, was very different from that in California. In the first place, Howard County is less urbanized than most California counties with jurisdiction over new communities. Second, unlike California, there are partisan elections at the county level in Maryland and, in 1962, the Republicans had unseated the Democrats in the election for County Commissioners, running on a platform which promised to increase minimum lot sizes from one-fourth of an acre to one-half. In other words, the electorate had recently expressed itself as anxious to stop or slow down growth. Third, the quality of public services in Howard County which, like most Maryland counties, has no municipalities, is far lower than those provided in California. Finally, Maryland law, unlike California's, has no provision for the creation of districts, except by act of the State legislature.

These conditions made Howard County much less favorable to a new community than such California counties as Orange (Mission Viejo, Irvine Ranch), San Mateo (Foster City), and Ventura (Janss/Conejo). Rouse felt that he must offer high-quality services in Columbia to meet his goals, but at the same time he deemed it necessary to guarantee Howard County that the additional costs for this would be borne by Columbia, not by other residents of the county.

While the work group and part of the staff engaged in planning, Rouse, Finley, Hoppenfeld, and the rest of the staff engaged in a continuous program of informal discussion about their intentions with residents and officials of Howard County. They stressed constantly their two-fold promise to build a community of high quality that would pay its own way. As the alternative to a new community such as Columbia (if local politics precluded its development), they held out the prospect of chaotic, urban sprawl. The road of negotiations in these discussions was a tortuous one, and there were times when partisan bickering as well as legal constraints seemed about to prevent Columbia from ever coming into being. The following paragraphs outline the modus vivendi finally worked out.

Informal discussions with County officials had indicated considerable opposition to a special tax district. Rouse and his staff saw great merit in allegations by County representatives that the creation of such a district would seriously impair the bonding capacity of the County. This might result in higher taxes to residents both of Columbia and of the rest of the County. Facing this and other drawbacks, as well as the likelihood of at least a one-year delay in attempting to get a district legislated into existence (for which local support was needed), HRD began to examine alternative mechanisms of easing its financial burden.

As of July, 1954, the favored plan was to create a non-profit association—the Columbia Park and Recreation Association. CPRA would have at the outset nine board members—seven from HRD and two ex-officio. As the development proceeded additional members would be elected to the board to represent the growing number of residents. By the time Columbia was substantially completed, the residents would have gained control of it.

CPRA would be empowered to undertake the financing, construction, maintenance, and operation of roads, walkways, parks, libraries, community service facilities, mass transportation, and energy-distribution systems. It would have the authority to issue securities (which Rouse believed could be marketed at reasonable cost eventually). CPRA would also be able to assess property, but there would be a fixed limit on the assessment of property not owned by HRD.

A nonprofit association may well be a useful device and the only one attainable under the circumstances. However, compared to such an entity as the Estero district at Foster City, it has the following potential drawbacks: 1) it probably would have to pay a relatively high interest rate; 2) the County probably would not assess and collect taxes for it as it would for a public entity; and 3) the possibility of securing grants (particularly from the Federal government) would be relatively low.

In November, 1964 the plan was submitted to the Planning Commission. HRD requested a planned community ordinance, but this met with considerable opposition, partly on grounds that this method was not appropriate under existing laws. Months of debate and discussion, during which Rouse appealed successfully to the general public through speeches and advertisements, produced a different approach which had the support of the Commission. This was a New-Town Ordinance, which would provide as follows:

1. The criteria for qualification (among them, that the minimum acreage be 2,500, and that all the property be contiguous);
2. Definite standards for minimum and maximum land uses (at least 20 per cent of the land would have to be in open space);
3. Procedures for regulating the height of buildings, lot sizes, coverage by buildings, and setbacks; and
4. Requirements for public water and sewer, public transportation, cultural, and recreational facilities.

In August, 1965, Columbia's preliminary development plan was approved by Howard County. Thus, Rouse is now able to cluster dwellings (homes, town houses, and apartments) on lots smaller than the otherwise required one-half acre, and devote the balance of the land to public uses, industry, recreation, open space, and commerce. Some observers feel that he has a commitment from the County not to grant zoning to anyone but him for the regional shopping center which is to serve the 300,000 people expected to live in and around Columbia.

Initial analysis by Rouse engineers as well as discusions with the Howard County Metropolitan District indicated that the cost of water supply and sewage-disposal facilities to launch Columbia would exceed $11 million. After much negotiation and engineering work, this figure was substantially reduced, and Columbia has been officially annexed to the District.

THE PLAN

As in California's new communities, the Columbia plan promises people a variety of urban services and recreation facilities, and the enhanced beauty of natural surroundings. As with El Dorado Hills and Reston (discussed in the next section), the plan calls for a series of villages each with its own "core."

Precise allocations of land to open space and recreation are not available for most new communities. A reasonably accurate general rule is that ten to fifteen per cent of the total will be devoted to such needs—part for activities such as golf, horseback riding, fishing and boating, etc.; and the balance for preserving the valley streams, steep hills, and wooded areas which constitute greenbelts. Columbia's allocation is the same as other new communities insofar as active recreation is concerned, but its amount of open land is greater—3,500 acres, or, over 20 per cent. This is so because the maximum over-all density set by Howard County's zoning ordinance is 2 units per acre as opposed to the zoning provisions affecting the Californians, an average of 3.25 units per acre. The percentage of land set aside for commercial and industrial use by Rouse is about the same as for the Californians.

In most ways, Columbia's plan is very much like those of the Californians, though there are several departures. The proposed Mom and Pop (or village) stores, and the mini-bus system are two of these; and as a third the plans call for parking to be shared in certain church, school, and store areas. But the most significant departure is the focus on an ambitious, multi-purpose town center. Often the Californians also plan for a town center but not one which aims to link together such a variety of facilities.

Plate 1 is a photograph of a model of Columbia's town center. According to the presentation made to Howard County,[22] the center will offer "a concert and music hall, docks for small sailboats and other craft along the shore of the lake, a town center park, a college campus, a hospital, and, in the evenings, the lights and sounds of the restaurants and cheerful cafes along the lakefront." In addition, the plan calls for the center to have regional shopping facilities, high-density housing, and office buildings. This concept of a metropolitan subcenter with a great variety of functions brought tightly together is a response to the urban-development critique, which has condemned the scatteration of such facilities in suburbia. In California, the general market forces and the desires of the managers of the various facilities in question both have helped cause such scatteration. As a result, community builders there have not held fast to their notions about compact centers. At Janss/Conejo, for instance, a site was sold to a Lutheran College several miles from the town center. If Howard County does not permit zoning for such uses on land adjacent to Columbia, Rouse may be in a stronger position to carry out this facet of his plan.

CONCLUSION

This description of the planning phase of Columbia has been essentially the story of one man's skill and dedication. James Rouse faced vastly more difficult problems in land assembly, political relations, and finance than did the Californians. Whatever the contribution of the work group to the

---

[22] *Columbia, A Presentation to the Officials and Citizens of Howard County, Maryland,* November 11, 1964, pp. 26–28.

actual development of Columbia, it must also be said that of all the community builders, only Rouse created such a group. He has already accomplished a good deal in assembling land, in making necessary political arrangements (aided by Finley and Hoppenfeld, whose experience in local government was of the greatest importance) and, most amazing of all, in securing funds for land purchase (and probably now also for development). Nevertheless, for Columbia to be a financial success and to carry out its innovations, it must still achieve a very rapid rate of residential and industrial sales. It may be that the same skill that Rouse has shown in inspiring confidence in himself and his ideas will enable him to accelerate sharply the usual rate of industrial growth. For example, if he can convince some large companies to locate installations in Columbia, this then will generate desire on the part of smaller plants. Installations of both sorts would spur the demand for housing, and this in turn would provide a demand for commerce. If all this happens, it will be much more the result of Rouse's efforts than of the virtues of Columbia's plan or of the planning process itself.

Reston

"The first residents are about to move into what promises to be one of the first modern communities in America worthy of its name." This is how a critic of city planning and suburban development, Wolf von Eckardt,[23] began an article on Reston, the most highly publicized new community and the only one which is attempting a major innovation in the design and siting of the housing itself.

Reston is the brainchild, and an extension of the personality, of Robert E. Simon, Jr., the son of a New York realty magnate. Before Reston, Simon's activities in his family's firm included the development of shopping centers in various parts of the nation. But Simon, always active in civic affairs, was restless

---

[23] *New Republic*, CLI, 19 (November 7, 1964).

with the mundane nature of conventional real-estate ventures. He had long been a devotee of modern architecture, and was especially taken with the plans and ideas of men like Clarence Stein, "Dean" of American city planners and designer of Radburn, New Jersey.

The Simon family's most famous holding was Carnegie Hall, which it sold early in 1961. Perhaps this sale served as a catalyst. In any event Simon decided soon after to put his ideas and his money on the line. On March 31, 1961, he purchased 6,750 acres[24] in Western Fairfax County, Virginia. The cost was almost $13 million. The site is about 30 miles west of Washington, D. C. The community that is in development there, Reston, is such a personal endeavor that its first syllable is made up of Simon's initials.

In his public statements Simon emphasizes the importance of the "developer's philosophy" and, by stressing the self-contained quality he projects for Reston, displays how the British New Towns have influenced him.

The beginning of a plan for a New Town must be a philosophy and not topography—not existing zoning and other ordinances of the community—not public financial regulations or other factors dealing with the money market. The developer must determine his own philosophy, select his objectives in order of importance and constantly insist upon preserving his program. Where an objective low on his list collides with one higher on the list, the less important objective must yield.

For Reston, the objectives in order of priority are these:

a. That the people who live or work in Reston can have the widest possible opportunity to use their full potential of mind and body;
b. That it be possible for any who want to remain in this single community to do so throughout their lives. Changes in circumstances of age, family composition, or financial situation should not make uprooting inevitable or even preferable;
c. That the importance and dignity of each individual be considered over the importance of the community.[25]

---

24 Later Simon increased this holding to more than 7,000 acres.

25 Paper given by Simon at the Anglo-American Seminar on the Planning of Urban Regions, Ditchley Park, Oxfordshire, England, July 17–21, 1964.

LAND, FINANCES, AND UTILITIES

Unlike Rouse, Simon had the initial advantage of having to deal with only one owner. For this original purchase, he made a down payment of $1.3 million, the balance due in ten equal, annual installments with no interest. However, Simon made no arrangements to secure additional funds either for future land payments or for utilities. It is likely that Simon underestimated the cost of utilities, and probably assumed that financing would not be difficult to find once the plans for Reston were prepared. We do not have precise figures concerning Reston's initial costs for sewer and water, but there is no doubt that, as for most new communities, they were substantial. Although much of the cost for off-site sewer and water lines is reimbursable to Simon by the two districts involved, either they could not or would not put up the money at the start.

Whatever the exact magnitude of these and other commitments, Simon soon had to secure additional funds, and he had considerable difficulty finding a patient and willing investor. After an extensive search, he secured a loan of $15 million from the Gulf Oil Corporation, to be amortized over a ten-year period at 5.5 per cent. This is a very low rate of interest even for a loan on a *short-term* real-estate development venture. Usually, unless a lender is given substantial security through a pledge of assets not related to the property, he normally would set a much higher interest rate for a project such as Reston. Part of the loan proceeds were used to retire the debt to the original owner so that Gulf could have a first mortgage. Gulf also received options on 40 service station sites and on 25 per cent of the stock in the corporation which owns Reston. It may be that these extra forms of compensation justified to Gulf the low interest rate.

Simon has been much less concerned with any change in political jurisdiction than Rouse or many of the Californians. He did not seriously consider either the creation of a district to finance services and facilities or the incorporation of Reston as a city. Fairfax County, with over 400,000 people, is reasonably urbanized and was receptive to the plan for Reston. Simon apparently believed that he could get sufficiently favorable treatment both on zoning and utilities to preclude the necessity of any change in political structure. Moreover, his commitment to a specific and unusual physical plan made him especially sensitive to the danger of giving any control over zoning to residents of Reston. Virginia law restricts incorporation, and neither the county nor the developer saw any reason to give up control to the early residents.

THE COMMUNITY

Although Simon had expressed interest in the social structure of Reston, his specific efforts in this regard were not as formalized as those of Rouse. Simon did not create a work group nor did he make great use of outside consultants to provide ideas about the possible institutions of Reston. He did, however, make much more of a commitment to "social planning" than did the Californians, and hired a full-time director for this purpose.

Reston's social planning director, Carol Lubin, has explained that the difference between the efforts at Columbia and those at Reston stems in part from the different geographic and social development in the areas in which the two cities are located. She notes that Howard County (Columbia) is a rural area with few services while Fairfax County (Reston), in contrast, has a variety of high quality, urban services which it has agreed to extend to Reston. Mrs. Lubin's task is to hasten the provision of these services and to encourage the County and private agencies to undertake special programs in Reston. As an example of the former, she cites the decision of the University of Virginia to provide adult education in Reston from the outset. She also cites a grant from the Educational Facilities Laboratory for an intermediate school in Reston designed to fit the needs of a growing community. Such special provisions are in addition to the variety of recreational facilities to be provided by the developer, which are basically the same as those provided by the Californians.

It is evident that the differences between the respective

political jurisdictions confronting each man accounted heavily for the greater emphasis which Rouse placed on institutional arrangements in his planning phase, however, the personalities of the two developers were equally important. Rouse never expressed any great interest in architecture for its own sake; in particular, he plays down the importance of design of the houses. His concern to create a better environment centered mostly on the provision of *non-residential* facilities and institutions in a small-town setting. Simon, on the other hand, sees a direct link between the quality of architectural detail and the social and spiritual lives of Reston's residents. Thus, though Rouse and Simon have similar images of the end result—a fairly self-contained town in which people not only can but will find enjoyment and stability—their methods for achieving the result are very different.

According to Mrs. Lubin, the ultimate success and value of Reston is very largely dependent upon industrial development. Slightly over 1,000 acres have been set aside for industry. As of July, 1965, sales or leases had been made to six companies[26] employing approximately 400 people and using about 13 acres. The largest of these companies (all research-and-development, or consultant firms) employs 115 people and occupies 5 acres. Such results, following more than a year of marketing and publicity, do not indicate that Reston's success with industry in the immediate future will be any greater than the Californians'.

THE HOME BEAUTIFUL

From the beginning Simon evidenced his special interest in design by hiring three prominent architectural firms—Charles M. Goodman and Associates; Cloethiel Smith and Associates; and Whittlesey and Conklin. Goodman and Smith both had extensive experience in urban-renewal projects, and each designed initial housing complexes. Whittlesey and Conklin drew the master plan, and also designed an initial housing complex

---

[26] Air Survey, Hazelton Laboratories, H.R.B. Singer, Human Science Research, Motorola, Transporation Consultants, Inc.

and village center. Thus, the first special feature of Simon's operation as compared with those of other community builders, was to employ architects to design the houses.

Plate 2 is a photograph of a model of the first village at Reston. The lake is man-made. The buildings forming the "J" in the foreground are part of the first village center. Designed by Whittlesey and Conklin, it contains stores, community spaces (above the stores), garden apartments (two stories) and a 16-story, 61-unit apartment building, the kind of high-rise building usually found in a dense, highly urban location. Such buildings are rarely built in a new area. The construction cost requires rentals for one- and two-bedroom apartments of from $150 to $300 per month. Probably few people will pay such rent in an area which is so newly developed.[27] The inclusion of this building in Reston's very first stage of construction (the building is nearly complete) is another testimony to Simon's desire to innovate architecturally—to achieve the visual and, incidentally, the demographic variety which suburbia has been condemned for lacking.

The houses at the top of the photo are by Cloethiel Smith. Those at the right are by Charles Goodman. Note how the units are clustered, leaving much of the land as common space. Conklin calls these complexes, "high density sinews." The housing arrangement, along with the road and walking-path systems, is intended to allow people to walk to the village center for shopping and leisure-time activities. In fact, the plan has provided for considerably less parking in this scheme than in the conventional layout, which regularly includes driveways, garages, and spaces on the street between driveways.

Plate 3 is a photograph of the Goodman and Smith houses as work stood in October, 1964. The photograph illustrates (and a personal inspection in June, 1965, verified) Simon's faithful compliance to the architect's plans.

As of July 1, 1965, construction was nearing completion on 227 town houses, the low- and high-rise apartments, and the village center. The first lake, a golf course, and club house

---

[27] Given development costs, even at these rents and at full occupancy, the return on the building will probably not be adequate.

were completed in 1964. In addition, about 150 lots of one-third to one-half acre in size (for more expensive houses) were being developed for sale to small builders.

In its industrial program, its recreation facilities, and its social planning, Reston represents a less ambitious break with the suburban past than does Columbia, and in these respects is not likely to be greatly different from California's new communities. The design, mix, and site planning of its housing are its true innovations. By far the most unusual of these (and the most important to the future of the development) has been the decision to make the majority of the housing units "suburban town houses"—two- and three-story attached houses in groups of four to ten at densities of from five to fifteen units per acre.[28] Of the total of 24,000 units, 17,000 are projected as town houses. (Of the balance, 4,000 are to be apartments and 3,000, detached houses.) Each individual lot is between 2,000 and 3,000 square feet. The balance of the land serves as common space for parking, roads, landscaping, and recreation. This common space is owned jointly by the residents of each complex, which at Reston is about 90 houses. (The detached, single-family houses which are the primary product in the early stages of other new communities, are usually set on lots of 6,000 square feet or more, and the average density is about three houses per acre.)

Recent experiences in California and in other parts of the nation, including Baltimore and Washington, suggest that town houses do not sell rapidly unless they are either less expensive than detached houses of comparable size or are in a location with a special atmosphere of its own. Examples of the latter are Pacific Heights in San Francisco, Greenwich Village in New York, Georgetown in Washington, D. C., and the developments immediately adjacent to the ocean in Los Angeles.

As to the price of the town houses, Reston (at least in the first stage) is certainly not offering a strongly competitive figure. The first of the houses have been selling from $23,000

---

[28] The term "suburban town house" is ours, though it is now in wide use. "Suburban" is used to distinguish these attached houses from those clustered together in central cities at very much higher densities.

to $46,000, prices which are higher than detached houses of similar size in locations closer to the capital. A development of town houses selling from $11,000 to $12,000 is now under construction near Reston and apparently is doing well. Thus, unless prices at Reston go down sharply later, which seems unlikely, prospective purchasers will have to decide whether its "esthetic" and "planning" qualities more than offset these deficits in traditional value.

We do not wish to mislead. The town houses at Reston are different from those in most cities in that much of the land saved by using small lots is transferred to local open space. Nevertheless, the early sales figures on the town houses have not been good. Further, there is considerable doubt that rental receipts from the high-rise apartments will be sufficient to offset costs. The individual lots, on the other hand, have sold very well.

From the beginning, Simon recognized that no merchant builder would risk his money on the kind of housing he wanted. Therefore, except for the detached units, he has his own organization (or has contracted) to build and sell the houses. His inexperience with this type of operation, the character of the terrain, and some characteristics of the houses themselves have all caused difficulty in this first phase of Reston's development. Recently, however, Simon has brought in three men experienced in the field of construction who may be able to eliminate some of these problems.

CONCLUSION

This then is a brief depiction of Reston, born of the desire of a man to show that "good" design and careful planning, as applied by an entrepreneur to the lovely Virginia countryside, would be judged favorably by the housing consumer and by suppliers of capital. If Simon can fulfill this desire, he hopes that Reston will act as a model proving to other developers that they can prevent "urban sprawl" and make money at the same time. That lenders and purchasers have not yet poured into Reston does not prove it may not be a success in the long run, financially and otherwise. Still, Reston's early difficulties may have a sobering effect on incipient community builders. Finally, if it does succeed in market and financial terms, there is the further question as to the impact it will have as compared to the developments of merchant builders on smaller parcels of land at fringe areas.

CHAPTER 5

Political Relations

CHAPTER 3 examined (in the California setting) the way in which urbanization and the government's response to it were important elements in making community building seem a financially worthwhile venture. We went on to observe in Chapter 4, that there has been a marked difference in the relations of community builders and merchant builders to governmental bodies, especially at the local level. Most local officials view merchant builders with considerable dislike and distrust, while community builders have received considerable cooperation and encouragement. The difficulties which James Rouse faced in Columbia, in creating a district and in securing zoning, illustrate how important the cooperation of a local government can be to the process of community building.

This chapter discusses in detail the three basic commitments community builders seek from government: 1) maximum freedom in zoning and subdivision regulations; 2) maximum influence over the location and timing of roads and freeway interchanges; and 3) authorization to create and control a district which will raise funds through the sale of tax-exempt bonds. A concluding section examines why, as a rule, community builders get what they want from local government in all three areas.

Zoning and Subdivision Regulations

The fundamental determinant of the value of a piece of land is demand, either by potential residents or by commercial or industrial users. However, during the past four decades, local government in the United States has gained increasing power to affect this basic market consideration by passing and administering laws which limit an owner's freedom in the use he can make of real property. Zoning laws and subdivision regulations now control such matters as the type of land use (residential, commercial, etc.), the size of lots, the width of streets, the height of buildings and their setback (minimum distance from property lines), and so forth. Though none of these controls can affect value if no demand exists, their influence can be great when it does.

As a rule, the value of land varies by its use. Proceeding from highest to lowest, the general scale of land values is as follows: 1) commercial sites; 2) land for apartments; 3) industrial sites; and 4) land for single family dwellings.

There are variations within each category. A site for a regional shopping center, expected to serve about 100,000 people and to have at least one major department store, is worth more per acre than, say, land for neighborhood services. Again, in any given residential zone (single-family dwellings and apartments) the higher the permitted density, the more valuable the land. Topographic and soil conditions, as well as the "market image" of any parcel, also affect value. Under many circumstances, despite the general pattern, apartment land is more valuable than industrial acreage. In fact, there is growing evidence that, in and of itself, land zoned for industrial use is not necessarily worth more than land zoned for residential use. But to a community builder it can be an important factor in creating demand for housing. Local employment raises the value of all the other land.

The following example demonstrates the significance of zoning to the land owner and developer.

From 1958 to 1963, the minimum lot size for detached houses permitted by Ventura County at Janss/Conejo was 8,000 square feet. (After 1963, the minimum limit was increased to 9,000 square feet.) An 8,000 square-foot lot allows slightly more than three lots per acre. During this period the median sales price to merchant builders for parcels of 50 to 100 acres with roads and utilities to their perimeter was about $10,000 per acre. Thus the cost of raw land per lot was about $3,000. Further, on relatively flat sites (less than 10 per cent slope) the per-lot cost of improvement was $3,000 to $4,000. Under these conditions finished lot cost averaged $6,500.

If the same land were zoned for lots 6,000 square feet in size, as is common in many cities and counties, the builder could get at least 4.5 lots per acre instead of 3. Assuming the land cost is constant, the raw-lot cost would be reduced from $3,000 to $2,200. Improvement costs would also go down by at least $1,000 per lot. Thus, a simple reduction in the minimum legal size of a lot simultaneously lowers its cost from $6,500 to less than $5,000. Certainly a 9,000 square foot lot is worth something more than one of 6,000, but not $1,500 more. Further, the builder can (in this example) increase his number of houses by 50 per cent with the same cash outlay for land and site improvements.

Obviously no land owner is likely to pass along such a benefit entirely to the builder. One would expect the average price per acre under these conditions to increase from $10,000 for 9,000 square foot lots to $15,000 for 6,000 square foot lots. The builder's cost per lot for land would remain about the same, but his cost per lot for improvements would be reduced. Thus, this kind of a change in zoning on a 100-acre parcel represents a difference in revenue to the owner of $500,000. These particular figures are somewhat arbitrary; they change from location to location and from time to time, but they are reasonably accurate and do illustrate the general relationships.

A land use potentially more valuable than houses is garden apartments. This usually means two-story structures with 20 to 30 units per acre. It is more difficult to assert a typical price for such land because fringe locations may have a strong market for single-family houses but not for apartments. Further, such land is ordinarily sold in smaller parcels requiring a greater outlay by the developer for site improvements. In a built-up area such as the San Fernando Valley or the San Francisco peninsula, 5- to 20-acre parcels sell at $40,000 or $80,000 per acre. Janss was able to procure garden-apartment zoning for 300 acres surrounding its town center and golf course. In 1964 Janss valued this land, and offered part of it for sale, at $25,000 per acre. As more industry moves in and the area generally becomes more urbanized, these prices will rise rapidly.

Industrial sites range from one to a hundred or more acres depending on the needs of the company. The average per-acre price in places like Irvine and Janss/Conejo is about $25,000. As with apartments, this must be adjusted in comparison with land prices for single-family houses because the developer must put in more site improvements.

The highest prices are paid for commercial property. In a neighborhood center land prices average $50,000 to $60,000 per acre. In a regional center they can exceed $100,000 per acre.

As indicated, land value is not solely the result of zoning. There must be an initial market demand or no amount of zoning for more compact or "higher" uses will make any difference. Nonetheless, planning authorities now tend to ration all uses of land except large lots for individual homes. This is especially true for regional shopping centers and high-density apartments. It is presumed that only so many such sites can be successful and that some control over them is in the public interest. Community builders have had great success in "preempting" these more valuable uses for their own land. With or without immediate demand, they have been able to get zoning for commercial and apartment use almost at will. As more and more new communities are initiated, it will be interesting to see if they will compete with each other before the county planning commission.

In addition to obtaining a potential increase in land value, some community builders have another, more particularized interest for getting their land variously zoned for industry, apartments, and commerce. This is to create so-called "income" land, which the user, after developing it, frequently rents rather than owns. Many community builders have considerable taxable income from other sources and, by owning not only a parcel of land but the buildings on it as well, he can get a much more favorable tax treatment on his income tax than if he were to sell the buildings. (This will be discussed more fully in Chapter 8.)

Community builders not only have sought more valuable

zoning, they have asked also that local governments be more flexible in applying specific zoning provisions and subdivision regulations. Traditionally, California cities and counties have attempted to establish clear regulations concerning both the kind of use to which land could be put and various elements of its development—setbacks (the distance of buildings from property lines), street widths, location of utility lines, and construction standards for site improvements, for example. Many, including builders and architects, have criticized the rigidity of such regulations. They have argued with increasing vigor that it stifles creativity and raises costs unnecessarily. Local government has answered with four points: 1) it is sound law to have clear regulations applicable to all equally (as opposed to administered criteria); 2) raising costs is in the interest of government, since the result will be higher values in general and, for itself, an improved fiscal position; 3) government does not have, and cannot get, the staff to administer complicated provisions; and 4) higher standards mean lower future costs for public repair and maintenance.

The proponents of greater freedom, including a few public officials like Roy Potter, Planning Director of the City of Fremont, have asked for "planned community" (PC) ordinances. In its ultimate form, a PC ordinance would provide that all statutory criteria may be disregarded if a developer submits a detailed plan. Elected officials or their designees, the planning commission and/or its director, would judge the plan solely on its own merits and in terms of the methods by which the developers would insure that it be carried out. There is probably no ordinance that goes this far, but a few California cities and many of its counties have adopted modified versions of the proposal. Two of the most interesting modifications, in Ventura and Orange counties, involved community builders.

At the beginning of 1963, the Janss Company had been operating for four years. Its relations with Ventura County had been quite satisfactory. In particular, the Company had gotten zoning for a regional shopping center and, by offering to dedicate over 200 acres of its land for a park (land too steep to be of great value), had gotten another 300 acres zoned for garden apartments up to three stories high and at a maximum density of 44 units per acre. This is known as an R-3 zoning.

However, the zoning turned out to present Janss with problems as well as an opportunity. In various ways—topography, parking, and setback regulations, and the market—the company was prevented from making maximum use of the land. The potential market was relatively small; much of the land was too steep to allow more than ten units per acre. Even on flat sites, parking and setback requirements would have prevented density of more than about 25 units per acre. Three-story structures were out of the question because renters would demand elevators, too expensive at such a relatively low density. Thus, the problem was: how could Janss proceed on sites which, during their early years of development, had to be suitable for low density, yet still apply creative design to all parcels, and ultimately gain the full value of the 44 unit per-acre density, or something close to it?

After some discussion within the organization and some informal talks with various members of the County Board of Supervisors and staff, Janss decided to draft a version of a planned community ordinance for adoption by the County. Originally, Janss' sole concern was the 300 acres zoned for garden apartments but, partly as the result of a request by the County, the draft covered all residential zones. This was to enable other developers to submit and the County to approve so-called cluster or suburban town-house projects at densities less than those permitted in an R-3 zone but greater than those permitted in an area zoned for detached houses.[1]

In general, Janss' ordinance provided that the Board of Zoning Adjustment could approve the use of land on the basis of a specific plan rather than on the basis of requirements in conventional zoning ordinances. However, the new ordinance set forth certain requirements of its own. It limited the over-all density of sites to 30 units per acre, and it required a con-

[1] Under its old ordinance, there was no way the county could approve a submission for housing at five to twenty units per acre. It either had to limit it to five (6,000 square foot lots) or permit garden apartments (44 units per acre).

struction sequence under which the average density of a given portion of the site at any time cannot exceed the maximum density.

At first glance, these provisions may seem unfavorable to Janss. For one thing, they reduce the company's allowable density on land already zoned from 44 units to 30. Further, since the average density can at no time exceed 30, Janss cannot even begin with a higher-density project at the outset.

But a closer look at the ordinance shows the potential advantages it gives to Janss. The market and topography of the land whose development problems led to the ordinance dictate that there will be no demand in the next few years for projects at a higher density than 10 to 15 units per acre. Some parcels will even be lower. Janss can begin development on these and simultaneously build up "credit" for the future. For example, if the first 200 acres are developed at an average density of 20 units per acre, a credit of 200 units and an average density of 50 can be applied to the last 100 acres. The ordinance, therefore, permits Janss (and others) to follow what is now the normal market pattern of building for higher densities as population increases demand. At the same time, the removal of some of the restrictions of standard zoning regulations allows Janss greater freedom in development and, in particular, will permit the company to build high-rise structures when and if the market arises for them.

Another community builder, the Irvine company, was also successful in gaining special zoning freedom under a planned community ordinance. The Irvines had been developing since the 1930's, doing most of their work along the coast. In 1960, they gave 1,000 acres to the State for a new campus of the University of California. At the same time, they hired William Pereira to do a master plan for 40,000 acres adjoining this land, a step that marked their decision to build one or more new communities. From 1960 through 1964 Irvine continued to plan and to lease land for development in Newport Beach. During this period the company was refining plans for a new community of about 10,000 acres around the new campus. In May, 1964 Irvine submitted to Orange County a plan for University Park, the first 1,000 acres of the community.

Unlike Ventura, Orange County already had both planned-community and planned-development ordinances. Under the former, a plan for a large holding can be submitted and adopted as part of the community's master plan. Under the latter, a plan can be submitted with or without the complete master plan, but it must contain the *specific design of buildings.* Irvine decided to seek provisions of a planned community and specify certain areas for planned-unit development. In some of these areas, land per house is planned at the minimum amount of only 2,500 square feet. In others, it is the more conventional 7,200 square feet per lot, but with no required front or side setback of the building from the property line.

In addition to these provisions for greater flexibility in residential site planning, Irvine also proposed specific sites for churches, schools, parks, commercial centers, a fire station, and so forth.

In San Mateo County the Fosters used an approach similar to Irvine by drawing a plan and having the County adopt it as part of the County master plan. In almost every new community, the developer does what is regarded as *public planning* and then submits his plan to the County for approval. There is little evidence that County officials have raised any serious objections to these plans.

Interchanges and Road Locations

We have already discussed the way in which new communities are frequently served by freeways planned and installed prior to (or at least without regard to) their development. To a lesser degree, the same is true of county roads. Community builders usually have been quick to perceive the importance of the location and timing of county roads and freeway interchanges. The following are some examples of the negotiation that has taken place over such matters. Individual quotations come from interviews or letters.

The Newhall Ranch, Valencia, is bisected by Highway 99, the principal route from San Francisco to Los Angeles through Bakersfield and Fresno. Highway 99 is now under construction as part of California's freeway program. Kerry Patterson, who directs the development at Valencia, provided the project with the following description of the relations between Newhall and the county and state in regard to the roadways.

We have been successful, and have had the Los Angeles County Engineers support in justifying five interchanges on this part of our Ranch—two of which are primarily for our development and one being provided in current contracts for roads not yet built.

This is more impressive when viewed in light of the fact that this is an Inter-State Highway project and that the California Division of Highways in turn has to justify these projects to the Bureau of Public Roads, which participates financially. We have also been informally integrating our major road network as it is emerging in our planning with the County Engineers. The County Engineer specifically and the Division of Highways, have been very cooperative.

One of the new interchanges is of special importance to Valencia. It will connect the freeway to a county road which not only will run through Valencia but will provide access to the freeway for some 30,000 people who already live in the area. As planned, the interchange will establish an excellent site for a regional (and later, town) shopping center, to serve both Valencia and the environs. This site is on the Newhall Ranch.

Another example concerns the San Diego Freeway now being constructed about 600 feet west of Mission Viejo. The developer's plan for the community included a four-lane, divided road with access to the freeway. But the 600 feet between Mission Viejo and the freeway might as well have been 6,000 miles, for the developers did not own the land and did not have the power of eminent domain. Further, 100 of the 600 feet is a main-line track of the Sante Fe Railroad, which could be crossed only by means of a bridge. Philip Reilly, Vice President of Mission Viejo Company, described what was done:

The road and bridge is now [January 15, 1965] under construction. This was accomplished by the County of Orange being "willing partners" to a limited degree. Mission Viejo Company entered into an agreement with the County to build the road and bridge at the company's expense. The County agreed that if Mission Viejo Company could not purchase the right-of-way at fair market value then the County would use its power of eminent domain. Since the right-of-way was a part of the Master Plan of Streets and Highways, this type of agreement was legally possible. Armed with this contract, which would prevent "blackmail prices" for right-of-way, Mission Viejo Company purchased the right-of-way and had it dedicated to the County. Mission Viejo Company then got the necessary permits from the Sante Fe, designed the road and bridge, and let the contract. The County has agreed to accept dedication of the road and bridge and will maintain it. Mission Viejo Company pays for all of the road and all of the bridge.

A third example involves Janss/Conejo, bisected by the Ventura Freeway which connects Los Angeles and Santa Barbara. It was vital to Janss that Moorpark Road, which serves the community's regional shopping center on one side of the freeway and serves specialized commerce (golf clubhouse, motel, shops) on the other, be an interchange. Further, in order to create more traffic for the shopping centers, it was desirable for Moorpark to be a major county road. The county had seriously considered putting such a major road well to the east of Moorpark. Janss' desires prevailed, partly because the company undertook to make a general road plan for the entire southeast section of the county.

The above illustrate both the importance community builders place on roads and interchange locations, and the substantial governmental cooperation they have had, mostly at the county level, in getting the roads they want. It should be noted, however, that this cooperation has not included any significant commitment of money on the part of government to build a road (or utilities) only to service a new community. The state and county road programs create a network which includes many new areas. The government willingly defers, though, whenever possible, to requests of community builders as to the exact location and timing of roads and interchanges. In much the same way, government has also provided major systems of water distribution for new communities.

Public Financing

Despite such assistance, there remain substantial outlays for infrastructure—streets, sewage disposal, and water distribution —which the new community must carry itself. Californians must frequently invest $10 million or more before any houses are marketable. At Reston and Columbia these early costs may be even higher. To finance such expenditures, the developer wants funds at low rates of interest and repayable only over a long period. But since a 4.5 to 5 percent loan with a 30-year term, say, is not normal business for a bank, many community builders seek the creation of one or more districts to finance their ventures. Several builders (Janss and Newhall among them) have enough capital to finance their own facilities, and prefer a private utility company rather than a public agency, for the profit they hope to make from hook-up charges and regular rates.

In allowing the districts to be formed, counties seem rarely to make a careful analysis of new communities to judge if they will be able to affect a sufficient rate of sale to service their bonds. (The bonds are secured only by the property, and are serviced by property taxes.) The presumption is that the under-writers and the bond buyers themselves make this judgment.

To date the most unusual governmental invention in matters of district forming is the Estero Municipal Improvement District at Foster City. This district has all of the powers of a municipality, with the exception of zoning authority and exercising of various police powers pertaining to enactment of regulatory ordinances of non-property, tax-revenue measures. It was created by a special act of the State Legislature and the District has been authorized to issue $72 million in tax-exempt municipal bonds which are secured by land and improvements. The debt service of these bonds is paid by property taxes levied each year; except that for water and sewer bonds net revenues are used, with the provision that taxes may be levied if needed.

The initial issue of $2.3 million was publicly bid upon only by the Republic Bank of Dallas, the Fosters' bank, which agreed to buy the bonds at par with the maximum interest rate of 6 per cent. There have been four subsequent issues totaling $42,820,000 with interest rates ranging from 4.5 to 5.6 per cent. As of January 1, 1966, there were $45,120,000 in bonds outstanding. The retirement of bonds varies from five years after issuance to 39 years as the maximum term.

The Estero District has three directors, one of whom is the manager. Two of the directors are selected by the property owners, and one by the Board of Supervisors of San Mateo County (in which it is located). Control of the District rests only with the owners of the majority of assessed valuation of the land. Present tax rate is $2.50 on a basis of 40 per cent valuation. The Fosters now project maximum indebtedness at $69 million.

There has been increasing concern at the state level in California about the multiplication of special districts, only a few of which actually result from community building. In 1963, the state legislature required the creation of a Local Agency Formation Commission in every county to pass on applications for annexation, incorporation, and the creation of districts. It is probable that legislation will soon be initiated to place further restrictions on district formation and to try to do away with some of those that already exist.

Also in 1963 the legislature authorized a new kind of entity, the County Services Area. In one respect this is similar to the Estero district in that the Area has the authority to carry out a number of functions. It differs from Estero, and single-purpose, districts in that the County Board of Supervisors, and not a board elected on the basis of assessed valuation, runs the Area. The possible effect of these changes on community building will be discussed in Chapter 7.

The View from the Government

From the perspective of the county official there are, or seem to be, very good reasons for the cooperative responses of government to the vital interests of community builders, behavior which is in such sharp contrast to the traditional view local government has taken of merchant builders and subdividers. An elected official must try to serve the welfare of the people. This means, among other things, raising property values, especially in suburban areas where a high percentage of the electorate are property owners. From the point of view of the local elected official, community builders serve the public interest in precisely this way for the following reasons:

1. Community builders own a great deal of land, the value of which they necessarily will try to raise. This means they will not bring in heavy industry or low-income residents.
2. Since they plan to be involved for a considerable length of time, they will follow through on promises to the county.
3. In contrast to many under-capitalized merchant builders and land developers, they seem financially capable of fulfilling their commitments.
4. Community builders have the expert staff and consultants to carry out their enterprise. (The fact that county officials take note of the particular consultants servicing a community may influence the builder in his selection of them.)
5. Community builders provide and manage facilities and services which would otherwise be the responsibility of the county, such as parks, swimming clubs, golf courses.

These various points can be illustrated by a representative sample of views of both government officials and community builders. From an Orange County official (speaking of the Irvine operation):

The huge developer has more capacity to make a better community. He can do good, orderly development . . . because he is large enough to hold on to most of his land while he carefully develops portions of it.
The County profits because, with one large developer, relations are simplified. Major land owners have a far-sighted attitude. They are also better able to dedicate sites for public purposes. They also give a quality product which produces revenue for the County.

A Ventura County official commenting specifically on Janss:

Janss is the best developer in the County and we are grateful they came rather than somebody else. It encouraged the whole valley to upgrade its design. Their long-term investment gives them good control and proper use of the location.

A Janss Corporation executive:

The Janss Corporation has great influence with the County Planning Department. Janss helped with the County's planned unit development ordinance which is now in use. It provided the engineering studies which later became part of general County plans and policies. Janss' support is important for the County staff when they go to the Board of Supervisors for a request.

A Newhall executive:

We are very happy with our relationship with local government to date. We are treated respectfully and sympathetically by the County [Los Angeles] partly because of our size and financial position.

Finally, an "outside" investigator, Frank Sherwood of the School of Public Administration, University of Southern California, has cogently summarized the essential basis of the interaction between local government and community builders in this way:

In part the big developer gets a different reaction from public officials because of his ability. In large part, however, he gets special treatment because the officials see him in terms of their own interests. Many communities have come to see subdivisions as liabilities. The advantage of a large developer is that he does not want to build low cost housing, and therefore will give a good financial return and a big image to the city or county . . . the public official will prefer the big developer with lots of talent and high standards every time.

A Concluding Note

In contrast to the Californians, Rouse experienced great difficulty in getting his plan approved; also, he was not given the authority to create a district. His difficulties stemmed from the differences in law and political climate between Maryland and California. In Maryland, county commissioners are elected as members of a political party (Democratic or Republican). In California, the elections are nonpartisan—a feature of the state's increasing professionalization of local government, in which county and city managers and planning directors play a larger and larger role in decision making. These professionals responded favorably to the proposals of the Californians, drawn and presented as they were by architects and planners who talked the same professional language. It was in part for this reason that the Fosters, for example, secured a special act of the State Legislature to create the Estero District. One reason for Rouse's failure to get special authority to create a district was that to do so he would have had to win approval both from a heavily Democratic legislature, and, from a Republican board of county commissioners.

California's long experience with growth has also made its residents less prone to enact highly restrictive zoning laws. For example, few California counties have large areas zoned for minimum lots of one acre or more, as is true in many eastern states. In this general respect, California's style resembles nineteenth-century America, when promotion of growth and settlement were national policy. No doubt there were "experts" in that era also who defended the country's policy of growth on economic and fiscal grounds. It is more likely, however, that this commitment to expansion—then and now—is not based on an actual analysis of monetary costs and benefits, but rather is part of what might be called the regional culture. People came to America to find new frontiers, so they still come to California. This attitude cannot help but affect public officials who promote great public programs on the one hand, and on the other restrain themselves from the ultimate exercise of restrictive power.

Given such a state of perceived mutuality of interest, it is hardly surprising that neither community builders nor county officials are eager to have early residents incorporate a new municipality. By creating a city, residents could place undeveloped land under their control, would have the right to zone, and might choose to interfere with the developer's plans. The community builder above all wants assurance that his vital interests—zoning and road locations—will not be subject to the capricious whims of those who might view him with disfavor. Since incorporation permits the new city to get sales taxes and subventions from the state, it might represent a fiscal advantage to local taxpayers. Nevertheless, we do not anticipate any push by community builders to have their land included in a new incorporation. If the residents initiate such proceedings, they will require approval of the Local Agency

Formation Commission. What its policy will be remains to be seen.

It might have been more entertaining for the reader (and ourselves) if this chapter had woven a tale of dark complicity between community builders and public officials. Bribery, rigged elections, and the harried supervisor tantalized by expensive wine and mysterious women are the stuff of political fiction, and often political fact as well. Fortunately—or unfortunately, depending on one's taste—there has been no sign of such behavior. The participants have simply not found it necessary.

CHAPTER 6

The Market

COMMUNITY BUILDERS see themselves as applying planning techniques to a large parcel of land. In market terms, this attitude rests largely on the assumption that by including amenities such as parks, lakes, golf courses, and community centers significant, unmet demand can be tapped. Such an outlook represents a distinct break with the behavior of merchant builders; although sometimes they have installed a few facilities, their chief activity has been to buy land at the fringe of a metropolis for the sole purpose of offering lower-priced housing than was available closer to the central city.

Few, if any houses in the communities, sell for less than $20,000; this is in part dictated by economics—specifically the cost of the land, of the necessary infrastructure (water, sewer, roads), and of the amenities cited above. But it is the result also of a conscious policy on the part of community builders in choosing the type of merchant builders to whom they sell land or lots. Each merchant builder tends to have his own style or type of operation. Some choose to build relatively inexpensive houses, others relatively expensive ones. Knowing this, community builders do not solicit offers from merchant builders who specialize in the "low end of the market" (even if such builders will pay the same price for the land as others). In addition, community builders stipulate verbally (and occasionally in contracts) the minimum price for which the houses to be built can be sold. To some degree, community builders have adopted these policies because of the urban-development critique, the brunt of whose attack has been upon the low- and moderate-priced housing of the merchant builder operating at the edge of the metropolis.

The purpose of this and the next two chapters is to analyze

104

and evaluate the behavior of community builders solely in market and business terms. In such terms, the decision first to increase the cost of the land by installing amenities, and then to affect house prices which are even higher than those the costs necessitate, rests on two assumptions about the market:

1. That in the areas around the new communities, there is no great demand for the kind of housing that can be sold for $12,000 to $19,000 and that people who want this kind of housing will not find the extra amenities a special attraction;

2. That people who represent the strongest source of demand for new communities—whose income falls in the $8,000 to $15,000 ($20,000 to $40,000 houses) range—will react more favorably to the community, at least during its initial years of development, if it does *not* contain lower-priced houses.

Neither of these assumptions is entirely novel, but the depth of commitment to them on the part of community builders is surprising—especially since it is clear that the assumptions are based almost always either on no formal analysis, or on occasional studies which were not highly reliable.

The Los Angeles Housing Market

To begin to estimate the validity of these assumptions, and to try answering these questions more reliably, Dr. Wallace Smith, at the request of the Project, analyzed the nature of the Los Angeles metropolitan housing market, with special emphasis on families earning less than $8,000 per year.[1] Los Angeles was

---

[1] Smith is an economist and Director of the Center for Urban Economics and Real Estate Research, University of California. His *Community Development Study—Market Analysis* will be published by that Center.

Smith was not able to provide a system of market analysis applicable to a single new community. Thus, techniques do not yet exist to make predictions about sales rates at given prices which are superior to the judgments of an experienced real-estate developer who constantly watches his own experience, that of competitors, and general economic trends. But Smith did provide the Project with a better understanding of the operation of the metropolitan housing market as a whole and confirmed, in general terms, the correctness of the community builders' decision to aim for the affluent market.

chosen because it is the location of so many new communities. Smith hoped to apply his general findings to Janss/Conejo, which had been on the market longer than any other new community. Specifically, Smith wanted to find out if Los Angeles contained a significant untapped demand on the part of families earning less than $8,000 per year for houses selling at less than $20,000, and whether Janss/Conejo in particular had failed to tap this demand. At the same time. Dr. Carl Werthman was asked to interview people who had already bought houses in Janss/Conejo and Foster City, a new community in the San Francisco area.[2]

It is now common knowledge that new housing is primarily built for those families earning more than the median income ($7,000 in California). In the past five years, a veritable deluge of reports declaiming this fact has poured out of public and private agencies. Not the least of these statements have been the demands of certain builders and developers for changes in public policy. In his study, Smith confirmed that the facts of the situation were as they had been reported:

> Examination of the income pattern of residential construction during the decade of the 1950's . . . in Californian metropolitan areas . . . clearly confirms an initial presumption that building is concentrated at higher income levels. In the Los Angeles metropolitan area, for example, 77 per cent of the increase in owner-occupied dwellings was accounted for by construction at income levels of $7,000 per year (the median in 1960) or over. A similar though less pronounced concentration is observed in the sales market in other California metropolitan areas, and in the rental market as well.

But Smith did not draw the standard conclusion from this information—that there is a great shortage of or unmet demand for housing for low and moderate income families. Rather, he presented the following argument:

---

[2] Werthman is a sociologist at the University of California. His study, *Planning and the Purchase Decision*, will be published as a separate book. Werthman's study supported developers' feelings about middle- and upper-income buyers' intolerance against those who bought less expensive houses. Even more important, he showed the perception or meaning of planning to be very different to the buyer than to the designers and their clients, the community builders.

It is often suggested that low-income groups are not served by the home building industry while high-income households have wide choice among new dwellings. This is a misleading impression. Correctly defined, the situation is more nearly the opposite of this commonly held view.

Smith maintains that one cannot analyze the housing market merely by asking what percentage of the new housing serves families of a given income. The housing market should be viewed as one in which people move through a given stock of units, made up in any short time period mostly of the existing supply of houses plus a small amount of new additions. Thus, the situation has been as follows: as income has risen, most new housing has served the needs of higher-income groups. While families with lower incomes (which also have risen) have gotten some new housing, most have been able to improve their condition by occupying used housing abandoned by the more affluent. Given the logic of these trends, it follows that if income continues to rise and if, as has been true, new housing units continue to exceed the combined total of family formations and immigration, ultimately the worst housing will be abandoned. (It is clear that not all lower-income families have participated in this "filtering" process, a matter to which we shall return in a later chapter.)

Forecasting the Los Angeles housing demand for the 1960-1970 decade on the assumption that income would increase at the same ratio as in the previous decade, Smith concluded that the "great bulk" of new demand would come from families earning more than $10,000.

Another way of judging the rationality of a market assumption is to ask the people who have direct business experience in the area. In 1964 interviews with six California merchant builders who, historically, had devoted all or most of their energies to building the least expensive housing possible under existing legal and cost conditions brought forth almost identical comments. Since 1959 or 1960, the prices of their cheapest house had risen from $500 to $1,000 per year. Further, the low-price models represented a decreasing portion of their total sales. A representative example comes from one builder who had sold most of his houses in 1959 in the $13,000 to $15,000 range. By 1964 his least expensive house was $18,000.

Part of this general increase, the builders explained, was attributable to rising costs, principally the cost of land and site improvements. The balance was due to improvements in the space and quality of the housing itself, changes that have been necessitated by changes in buyer preferences. "We cannot sell a minimum house," said one builder, "because people demand more features like shake roofs and built-in appliances."

All the builders further agreed that families who could not afford new houses were buying used houses, or renting houses or apartments. An increasing percentage of the new house buyers were moving to within a radius of five to fifteen miles of their former homes, thus leaving them empty for lower-income families.

These assertions suggest that builders no longer can compete with used houses on the basis of price but must offer *more* space and quality. Between a new minimum house and a used house, most families see the latter as a better buy. This situation is no doubt influenced also by the way in which jobs are distributed. Most employment opportunities in California for blue-collar and clerical workers exist near the supply of used housing. A sizeable percentage of employment in the fringe areas, where there is land for new housing, is in the higher-paying job categories.

For various technical reasons, Smith was unable to apply his general findings about Los Angeles to Janss/Conejo, or to develop a system for doing this. So it is difficult to say with any certainty whether this new community deviates substantially from the general trend. What evidence and information we have are somewhat conflicting.

Smith maintained that since Janss/Conejo is connected by freeways to a large number of employment centers within 45 miles, the market conditions of that community most probably mirror those of the metropolis as a whole—in other words, that Janss/Conejo was *not* ignoring a strong potential market for its homes. Others, however, have argued that at the very least the community was overlooking the demand that existed among

PLATE 1. A model of Columbia's town center.

PLATE 2. Lake Anne Village, the first village at Reston.

PLATE 3. The Goodman and Smith houses at Reston.

the lower-income population who worked in the stores and plants nearby. This argument claimed that such people were commuting from San Fernando Valley or some other area which offered the used housing they could afford.

To try to find out if local employees were in fact commuting in, we mailed a questionnaire to most of the employers in the Conejo area requesting the following information: 1) the length of time the firm or plant had been in Conejo Valley; 2) their total number of employees; 3) a male-female breakdown of employees; 4) a breakdown by annual income—under $6,000, from $6,000 to $8,000, and over $8,000; and 5) a breakdown, by place of residence—Conejo Valley, another part of Ventura County, San Fernando Valley, and any other part of Los Angeles County.

We received replies from 209 firms with 4,950 employees, 3,086 men and 1,864 women. Only 42 companies (totalling less than 900 employees) had been in the area before 1960. The smallest of the companies had less than 10 employees and the largest 1,502. Over 60 per cent of the men and more than 95 per cent of the women earned less than $8,000, the minimum amount needed to buy a house in Janss/Conejo without a large down payment. Over 30 per cent of the men and 85 per cent of the women earned less than $6,000.

Despite the preponderance of employees earning less than $8,000 per year, few of them were commuting any great distance. Excluding one company which had moved from San Fernando Valley so recently that its employees could not yet have moved in great number, almost 80 per cent of the men, and over 90 per cent of the women lived within a commuting time of approximately twenty minutes. Over 50 per cent of the men and almost 70 per cent of the women lived in the immediate area of Conejo Valley itself. One firm reported 30 (out of 32) employees earning less than $8,000, 27 of whom were earning less than $6,000. Yet out of the total 32 all but three lived in Conejo Valley.

On the surface these data seem irreconcilable with the sales prices of homes at Janss/Conejo. How can people with such low incomes buy new houses priced at over $20,000? The presence of some of these people may be accounted for by the purchase of older homes in Conejo Valley; some may depend on the rentals of the few apartments in the area or the purchase of new homes in the Conejo Valley outside of the Janss land, where there have been a few small housing projects. Although the hard evidence to document the point completely is lacking, it would seem that most of these lower-income employees are part of a family with more than one wage earner, so that the total family income is sufficient for the purchase of a home in Janss/Conejo. It may well be that a selective process is taking place in fringe locations whereby lower-paying jobs are filled by people who are the second earner in a family. It does seem fairly clear that the Janss community in particular is not losing great numbers of such families to lower-priced homes further away.

As to the significance of all these data on the question of whether community builders in general have rational pricing policies, the situation appears to be that they have over-reacted to a trend. Incomes have gone up; filtering is taking place; and no doubt the people who want a better house in a better environment are willing to pay something extra to get it. But there is a limit to how much they will pay. If the biggest demand ten years ago at the edge of the California metropolis was for houses selling from $13,000 to $16,000, it is now probably for houses selling from $17,000 to $25,000. This is illustrated by experiences both at Janss/Conejo, where houses put on the market in 1964 at $17,000 to $22,000 have vastly outsold the higher-priced houses, and at Foster City, where the less-expensive houses ($23,000–26,000) sell much more rapidly than more expensive units. The assumption made by some community builders that demand will *not* drop swiftly with rising prices seems to us erroneous.

Planning and the Purchase Decision

In examining the assumptions of community builders about their market, three questions presented themselves:

1. What are the trends in housing demand in terms of income?
2. Do buyers in new communities interpret "planning," including the material amenities, in the same way the planners and community builders do?
3. What effect would the inclusion of lower-priced houses have on the demand for those selling at more than $20,000?

Smith, as seen in the preceding pages, dealt with the first of these questions. Carl Werthman sought the answers to the last two in interviews he conducted with residents of two new communities, Janss/Conejo and Foster City. He was asked to interview people who had already bought homes in Janss/Conejo and Foster City, a new community in the San Francisco area. The community builders had expressed fears that the inclusion of lower income families in their developments, even in separate subdivisions, would drastically impair sales to the more affluent, and presumably larger, market. Werthman's first task was to test this hypothesis by examining the degree of tolerance toward lower income families felt by people who already lived in the developments. Further, since community builders considered "planning" their fundamental function, he was to examine the role it played in the purchase decision.

City planning is normally thought of as a process in which trained professionals map out a piece of land, designating the areas to be devoted to roads, parks, housing, commerce, schools, churches, industry, etc. It is presumed that such professionals have the knowledge which enables them to determine the best way to allocate the land, given its topography and certain assumptions about its expected rate of development. The urban-development critique held that such planning—planning, that is, prior to development—would produce an environment vastly superior to one created by developers and merchant builders who, dealing with fragmented pieces of land, could not or would not follow the advice of a planner.

Community builders not only have accepted the validity of this thesis but have gone on to assume also that the buying public either recognized, or could be made to see, the advantages resulting from comprehensive planning. In other words, community builders believed that they and the professionals, on the one hand, and the prospective consumers, on the other, all saw planning and its virtues in the same light. Werthman's main task was to find out whether this was so, whether planning as such was what consumers understood as planning.

Werthman conducted his study in two phases. During the summer of 1964, he tape-recorded a series of long, semi-structured "depth" interviews in the houses of residents at Foster City and Janss/Conejo. Altogether there were 74 interviews, 30 from Foster City and 44 from Janss/Conejo. In addition, Werthman conducted 17 interviews with homeowners living in subdivisions immediately adjacent to Janss/Conejo, and 11 more with people who had looked at homes there but had chosen not to buy. Thus, in the first phase of the study, he had a total of 102 "qualitative interviews," each, when transcribed, between 15 and 30 pages long.

On the basis of these interviews, Werthman designed a detailed questionnaire consisting largely of multiple-choice items. The questionnaire was distributed to 125 of the 180 families then living in Foster City (the remainder were either not at home or had participated in the earlier phase). One hundred and nineteen questionnaires were returned. In Janss/Conejo about 900 questionnaires were distributed and 670 returned.

From his analyses of the interviews and the questionnaires, Werthman concluded that there were characteristics of a new-community house on which the decision to buy was based. The first of these is what he terms location, which includes the relationship of the community's site to other parts of the metropolis (such as the major commercial and entertainment activities), the relation to the buyer's job, and the general physical condition of the site (climate, topography, and so forth). All the factors which contribute to the element of location have one thing in common: they are entirely beyond the control of the developer. He cannot produce a better climate, lessen the amount of smog, change the site of employment centers, or reroute a highway.

The second element involved in the decision to buy is the space and quality of the house. This is subject to some control on the part of a developer. If he designed and built the house, as merchant builders do, he would have considerable discretion as to the size and number of rooms, the material, and other features. But, as already explained, only Robert Simon at Reston is attempting to do this. Thus, what influence community builders exercise in this area is through their selection of particular merchant builders. But such control seems to produce no significant differences in the quality of the housing in a new community as opposed to housing put up on land being developed under fragmented ownership.

The third element pointed to by Werthman, and the one which community builders see as their principal contribution, is what he calls "community"—the total environment. It is at the "community" level that the planners and sponsors of these large projects believe they are changing the nature of suburban development.

Using the word "community" to refer to the results of planning, Werthman argues that the most important attribute of a community is its "class image," which stems from "a combination of various elements in the physical environment that symbolically identifies or expresses the relative social status of community residents to the rest of society." The class image of a community, according to Werthman, varies directly with the extent to which the community appears to minimize certain risks. "The residents all agree," he writes, "that the essence of 'planning' is control and that its major benefit to the home owner is freedom from the anxiety associated with personally uncontrollable change."

Such control, or the reduction of risk, can come about in different ways. If one buys a house in a neighborhood whose character has remained unchanged for a long time, or whose direction of change has been constantly favorable, the purchaser takes this as strong presumptive evidence about the future. If the governmental jurisdiction has a precise plan and has shown itself ready to enforce that plan, the future becomes more predictable. In a new community, where usually there is a great deal of open land and where the rates of change can be rapid, uncertainty can be kept to a minimum only under three conditions: 1) the surrounding land must be owned by one person or company; 2) the owner must have a sound reputation; and 3) the owner must present to the buyer a detailed plan for the land adjacent to the house being considered. These conditions represent a kind of definition of community building.

Community builders and planners were not unaware that buyer were quite concerned about this element of risk, but in their press releases, advertisements, descriptions of their plans to public authorities, and comments in interviews, they have manifested a strong belief that people interested in new communities also wanted to have access to various kinds of facilities, especially for recreation. For example, the brochure for Foster City is packed with references to the opportunities for boating created by the community's system of lagoons. Janss/Conejo's sales literature cites the variety of available activities which add up to "the sporting life." A resident can "play 18 holes of championship golf after breakfast, ride a horse after lunch, take kids for a hike in the afternoon and finish off with a few games of bowling."

Werthman found, however, that few residents of the Foster City or Janss/Conejo expected to make great use of the major recreational facilities of the community. Only 16 per cent of the respondents from Foster City said they expected to use the lagoons often, and only 7 per cent from Janss/Conejo expected to use the golf course often. On the other hand, these responses do not mean that the recreational facilities had no effect on the purchase decision or, at least, on the buyers' perceptions of the community. Of the respondents in both Foster City and Janss/Conejo, 90 per cent said that the facilities "added to the general atmosphere."

From the buyers' viewpoint, then, one basic purpose of "planning" in a new community is to minimize the insecurity that surrounds such a venture. More specifically, "planning" will prevent certain negative possibilities, and insure certain positive conditions—for one, the "class image" (as Werthman calls it), created by the price of nearby homes. Werthman illustrates the point by quoting the following two responses:

You put a house like this in with a lot of other houses just like it and who cares about it? It doesn't look any better than it is. But you put it in with more expensive houses and it looks like a lot better house. Over there, not more than two blocks away, there are houses that are twice as expensive as this one, so when someone comes to look at this house they think it must be good because look at the rest of the houses around here.

You have your low class people and your high class people, but over here we are medium or upper medium class and I just like it better. The tract itself was nice. It was just its surroundings. On one side you had Starview which is very expensive and on the other side, not too far away from you, you had custom houses. But also not too far away were those very cheap houses that were not well kept at all and the people were a very low class, and I would rather be over here.

"Planning" also has to do the whole visual appearance of a community—what Werthman calls its "social esthetic" ("social because the arrangements are used symbolically to organize relationships between people and esthetic because the medium used to symbolize those relationships is essentially visual").

In this community they had all the utilities buried underground, we were right on top of a hill, we had a magnificent view that wasn't marred by telephone lines, electric light cables and what-have-you. Every house was individual. Trees had been left, and there was a big wall all around the estate so there was only one entrance to all the houses through the gate, somewhat like the idea they have in Bel-Air [an upper class development] though not in that class. But it made such a tremendous difference.

I think one of the bad parts is that as you came down into it [an area of low priced homes, which Janss/Conejo respondent thought of as inferior to his own location], all you can see is a long flat area—the valley floor—I never got to the sides, to the foothills, but all I got was this impression of a jungle of cracker-box houses —not really—but they gave that appearance from their similarity, their lack of any landscaping such as the trees they have in the Thousand Oaks area. Seems that all I could see was a jungle of telephone poles and utility wires. I just didn't like the atmosphere, there didn't seem to be much planning as far as shopping centers were concerned.

In addition to protecting (and, on occasion, improving) one's class image, "planning" also serves to maintain one's monetary investment. These several functions tend to become inseparable. A home buyer knows that people in general expect to be judged by the condition of their houses and their settings, no matter how he may feel individually about such a method of social definition. Thus, if he is at all concerned about the resale value of his prospective house, he must necessarily concern himself with the financial prospects of the entire community. Some residents of Janss/Conejo and Foster City saw "protection of investment" as decreasing the likelihood of a loss of their equity (down payment) upon resale, but the majority interpreted the phrase to include reasonable assurance of a profit. For example, approximately a third of the residents in each community expected their home to rise in value $1,200 per year or more. Almost 50 per cent thought annual appreciation would be between $500 and $1,200. One Janss/Conejo resident told how important investment considerations were in the buying process:

> Primarily in buying a house here, we weren't looking for a house that would send us but for something that would be a good investment. There are, of course, a lot of features we were looking for, but the most important over-all factor would be investment. We wanted something we could sell for a profit in a few years after we have lived here awhile.

For the buyer in a new community, the essential role of "planning" is to maximize the potential appreciation of his investment. The following comment illustrates the point:

> There will be restrictions. There won't be any high wires. You won't look out and see trailers, and no big trucks. It will be nice and quiet. They won't allow people to tear the place up. They will have to take care of their houses and yards. Keep it nice looking. We would have bought the house anyway but it just made it easier to make up our minds faster 'cause there will be plants and nice yards that will cause the value of this house to increase.

It became clear that this view of "planning" was closely bound up with the question of the degree of tolerance which residents of Janss/Conejo and Foster showed toward lower-income families. "Planning" to these residents was a guarantee against the introduction of "undesirable" elements close to one's house and immediate surroundings. Not surprisingly, the most undesirable were lower-priced homes inhabited by lower-income people.

> [Would you mind if a neighborhood of houses selling for $18,000 were built in Janss/Conejo?] Yes, I would. Because I think when you

think of Janss/Conejo you think, "Oh that's me." We are part of it and then you think well, I'm afraid it would look just like it does across the street. When you get those people, it is kinda like paying rent. They get in for nothing down, dollar down. That's what I don't want to see. When people have to put something into a house, it's not the price, I don't think that makes the big difference, it is how much people have to put into it that determines who moves in. And if you only have to put a dollar down you get anybody.

I understand there's some areas in San Jose where new homes are for $10–11,000, they put these tract homes with VA, no money down, and what the hell, he's getting a new home; that's all he cares about and he lets it run down. That's why I guess if a guy puts more money into a house he takes better care of it. People are people. If they're the type that don't take care of a place and don't like to have their yard look nice, and don't keep their house clean, you can put them in a $100,000 home and they'll ruin it.

Sixty-nine per cent of the respondents in Foster City (where the less-expensive homes range from $23,000 to $26,000) said they would oppose including a neighborhood of $20,000 homes even if it were separated from other neighborhoods by a lagoon and a row of apartments.

Most residents of both communities emphasized poor maintenance as an adverse result of nearby lower priced homes. As one Foster City owner put it:

I think the people in this community are going to take pride in their homes because they are middle class. If this were in the class of say $9,000 or below, it would be different. In your $9,000 income or lower, the poor guy is worked to death and he ain't got time to get out in the yard. It's not that they care less, it's simply that the next door neighbor doesn't give a damn and pretty soon he's convinced he don't give a damn either. Yet you'll get a few out of the bunch that will take care, but in the long run it will all go down.

The "poor" are not the only undesirable element which "planning" must guard against. Industrial plants, offices, and stores must also be kept away from homes. Protection from all these elements, particularly the less affluent, as a function of "planning," was underlined again and again by comparisons that Janss/Conejo residents made between their circumstances and the conditions facing homeowners on the other side of Moorpark Road, a boundary line of the community. In the area across the road there are several small subdivisions and shopping complexes undertaken by different builders.

I think we liked this side of Moorpark Road much better. The fact too that on the other side of Moorpark Road the homes are much cheaper. You hardly have to put anything down and you just don't get as NICE PEOPLE on that side as you do in this tract.

. . . in the other section [across the road] they have some beautiful custom houses, but the roads are really quite bad and it just isn't planned. You see beautiful custom houses, a nice cluster of them, and then you have a rundown home and then there is a few acres of nothing.

This is strictly a feeling I have, but it seems to be that, first of all, it [Janss/Conejo] seems to be more of a planned community . . . this is planned. This is not just thrown together. It's not just throwing a bunch of houses together. . . . It is in a way, but not so much as other tracts. I don't know exactly how they work, but there's one group that has some control over what happens. I would think that this would increase the value of the homes, if they control it somewhat. . . . They are selling an atmosphere more than any other tract that I know of. [What things give you this impression?] Well, one thing it seems like most people take pride in their homes and keep them up. They have nicer yards. [Was this important to you?] Yeah, for the resale value. If my neighbor has his place looking nice, then mine is going to be worth more.

One might summarize the effect of "planning," from one viewpoint, as an attempt to insure people equally against negative knowns and unknowns. This insurance is made credible both by a developer who owns the surrounding land, who is capable of and committed to the development of that land, and whose self-interest will not be served by the introduction of "undesirable" elements—and by a detailed "plan." At Janss/Conejo (which presented buyers with a far less detailed map of the community than did Foster City) the mere fact that the developer was Janss—well known for its development of Westwood, a high status area surrounding UCLA—combined with the fact that the Janss family owned the land, was "planning" enough.

Conclusion

To what extent, then, are community builders by-passing a market for homes priced lower than $20,000? Relying partly on Smith's analysis of the Los Angeles housing market and also on our interviews with merchant builders (as well as on some supplementary material), it seems to us that community builders correctly perceived a tendency in their initial market but now have overreacted to this trend. Projections indicate that the strongest demand for housing in fringe locations will continue to be at the lower end of the current spectrum of price ranges being offered. However, as incomes have risen and the housing shortage has receded, the whole spectrum has shifted so that a lower-priced house in 1965 is $17,000 to $20,000 while in 1955 it was $10,000 to $15,000.

As to how residents of a new community understand the meaning of planning and their level of tolerance for lower-priced housing, it is clear now that the two questions are inseparable. Planning turned out to have a very different meaning, albeit an important one, to buyers than to professionals, including community builders. To the buyers, "planning" essentially means conditions or actions which minimize the risk that identifiable or unknown changes would present to their social image and their monetary investment. The change most feared by residents is the construction of markedly less expensive housing nearby.

Some observers have challenged conclusions drawn from only two communities and statistical analyses based on only one metropolitan area, Los Angeles. It can be said in regard to Werthman's study that Janss/Conejo and Foster City are in different parts of California and relate very differently to their respective metropolitan areas. Werthman shows the significance of these differences as well as the differences in the behavior of the respective developers. His techniques and conclusions appear to have considerable validity as applied to other situations. However, the confinement of the Project largely to California must be taken into account by the reader. The findings of Werthman and Smith certainly affected greatly the analysis and conclusions in this book.

CHAPTER 7

Community Building as a Market and Political Strategy

As NEW COMMUNITIES move from a general idea to a project which must be financed, approved by government, and sold, community builders come to see their activity fundamentally as a marketing and political strategy. This does not mean that they are no longer concerned with the task of attempting to present an alternative to the ostensible evils outlined in the urban-development critique, but just that the political and financial requirements of community building now become the major issues with which they must contend.

The two preceding chapters focused, respectively, on the nature of the political relations and the pricing policies of community builders. This chapter will begin an evaluation of these activities.

As already indicated, community builders see themselves as being superior to other kinds of developers because they have the resources and the *will* to engage in long-run physical planning. The general meaning of planning, whether for a new community or for any other enterprise, implies taking into account future problems and opportunities before they become immediate issues. Yet what a study of the planning activities of community builders reveals is often just the opposite and, in fact, a general unawareness of problems more or less inherent in the community-building process which developers may have to face.

Market Strategy

Many community builders seem to have assumed that the effects of their physical planning would become the dominant factor in the purchaser's decision, sometimes even that it could outweigh serious deficiencies in location or overcome adverse conditions in the housing market. There is simply no other way to account for such new communities as El Dorado Hills or Sunset/Sacramento. Both are about thirty miles from the center of Sacramento, with a great deal of unused land between them and the city, as well as in other parts of the metropolis less distant from its center. In addition, ever since the mid-1950's, the housing market in the Sacramento area has been characterized by high-vacancy rates and over-building. The area is and has been a "soft market." Given this background, it is no surprise that the rate of sale in both new communities has been very slow. Whatever their developers had hoped or anticipated, the planning, and physical attributes of the sites themselves have been insufficient to cause any dramatic change in consumer behavior.

These lead to certain conclusions about the way market analysis bears upon the community building process. First, the builders' expenditures for consulting firms, whose job it was to predict the absorption rate at varying price levels, has been largely wasted. In part this waste has simply been the result of community builders' refusal to heed the information and advice they received. But, more important, it is also due to the fact that there do not now exist any techniques for market forecasting which are any more reliable than the judgment of an experienced developer or analyst who does little more than keep detailed track of current market behavior. In other words, the willingness of a builder to pay a consulting firm a large fee does not mean the builder thereby will add much, if anything, to his ability to make long-run judgments about demand. Merchant builders sometimes use research firms to supplement their own sources of information, but most of them are skeptical that this promises easy answers. Community builders have been much less skeptical. Some of them (to put the matter bluntly) have even adopted a system one might call "cost determinism," in which one calculates the cost and the rate of sales and prices which must support that cost, and then assumes that that is what the demand is.

Community builders have also been slow to question the ability of architect-planners to keep costs within reason and at the same time make what is good planning as such become good "planning" to customers. Even after instances in which one has been able to observe the lack of strong market response to a community and the wide distance in attitudes between consumers and planners, subsequent community builders have continued to employ the same misinformed and misinforming consultants.

This general tendency on the part of community builders not to be incisive about the market is evidenced by their substantial failure to consider the sort of paradoxes suggested by Werthman's study, readily apparent to anyone who takes a close look at the residents of a new community. These paradoxes have to do with the difference between planning and "planning," and with differences in the relative weights to buyers at various price levels of "planning," location, and the house itself.

It follows from Werthman's conclusions—that the essential role of "planning" is to insure against negative knowns and unknowns, and that the most important negative factor is lower-priced housing nearby—that prospects for higher priced houses will demand "planning" more than other buyers but that their wishes also will be more difficult to satisfy. In addition, their ability to pay more enables them to select communities in which risk is minimized by the existence of older houses of similar price and by the absence of vacant land or any factor threatening instability. This is illustrated by some data on Janss/Conejo.

Janss/Conejo has the locational *disadvantage* of distance (it is at the edge of urban Los Angeles) and the locational *advantage* of cleaner air and cooler summer temperatures than most of the Los Angeles area. It has the further locational advantage, to some people, of scenic beauty and of not being crowded. Without the existence of the Janss family as a large land owner and/or of a detailed plan, it would have had the "planning" disadvantage of high risk, because buyers would have been unsure of the future of the surrounding land. Thus, "planning," while important, only becomes a factor if the locational advantage is seen as appealing. Eighty-seven per cent of the buyers of the highest priced homes at Janss/Conejo said that outdoor atmosphere, weather, and natural attractiveness together constituted one of the two most important reasons for buying. This was true of less than 50 per cent of those buying the least expensive homes.

As Werthman has defined it, "planning" is most advantageous for buyers of lower-priced houses ($18,000 to $22,000), since all the surrounding homes are more expensive. *But the most important factor in the purchase decision to the buyers of the less expensive homes seems to be space and construction quality.* When asked what were the two most important reasons for buying, approximately 65 per cent of the buyers of low- and medium-priced homes said space and construction quality. Only 25 per cent of the buyers of the highest-priced houses responded this way. If it is correct to judge that the principal source of demand in a fringe location is from prospects for $17,000 to $25,000 houses, community builders are presented with a possible dilemma: Will the additional cost of planning and amenities prevent them from capturing this market? Are their pricing policies, which attempt to offer guarantees to buyers of higher priced homes, resulting in a greater loss of sales rather than gain?

Now, there are no clear answers to such questions. They represent a problem, common to any business, in the trading off of possible benefits and losses. In this context, however, the main point is the reluctance of community builders to view such issues in these basic business terms.

Two additional paradoxes illustrate the same approach, or lack of one. The first concerns the matter of scale. If the essential role of "planning" is assurance about the surrounding area, how large an area is involved? The size of new communities has resulted partly because of the amount of land owned and partly because of the desire to get zoning for certain uses, especially a regional shopping center. Is it conceivable that one could negotiate the necessary zoning for a site of 10,000 acres or more but present to prospective purchasers a plan for only 2,000 to 3,000 acres? Scale becomes a particularly important consideration as soon as one raises the issue of whether customers will treat changes in the plan with which they are presented as broken promises on the part of the developer.

This problem arose at Janss/Conejo. Janss reduced lot sizes from one acre to one-half and one-third acre in Lynn Ranch, a part of Janss/Conejo. In addition land nearby was sold to the North American Aviation Company for a Science Center. The Science Center was built to house physical scientists who needed a place to think, and North American explicitly desired that it be near a residential rather than an industrial area. It is difficult to believe that a building surrounded by landscaping and housing Ph.D.'s will seriously disrupt the lives of Lynn Ranch residents. The same can be said of one-half to one-third acre lots. Nevertheless, many of the early homeowners were upset. As one put it: "There have been things completely opposite from what it was supposed to be, like the Science Center. It went up in a residential area."

The community builder is further faced with the fact that many residents blame him for the faults of a merchant builder. One group of houses in Janss/Conejo bore the brunt of a number of such complaints. In analyizing the situation, Werthman[1] writes:

Many of the mistakes made by individual builders are eventually blamed on the developers. The most widely held conception of planning, at least in the eyes of the respondents, is based on the assumption that the developer has ultimate power, and thus farming out work to builders involves a risk. Should potential buyers become aware that in fact developers have little control over builders, they would certainly be inclined to lose faith in the plan and the developer. Perhaps the most interesting thing about complaints from this subdivision, however, is that people somehow never quite believe that there is nothing that the Janss Corporation can really do about their problems with the builder. They may curse the Janss Corporation for not caring but never for being out of control.

Awareness of this problem has led some community builders to try to exercise great care in the selection of merchant builders

---

[1] Werthman, *op. cit.* See Chapter 6, footnote 2.

and in policing their practices. Provisions requesting submission of plans for architectural review, minimum square footage, and minimum sales prices have been established, though it is difficult to draft agreements which can be legally enforced.

Despite the difficulties which stem from dealing with merchant builders, community builders do not seriously question the practice. This seems due to their lack of recognition that in certain situations costs and benefits must be weighed. Community builders have not tried to ascertain the effect of less than totally satisfied buyers upon future prospects. Morality aside, what difference will it make in the rate of sale? Werthman writes:

If we can assume . . . that people who live in planned communities are also a principal source for potential buyers, then we can also conclude that "faith in a developer" or "faith in a plan" cannot be breached without peril. Given the way new home buyers define the appeals of "planning," to betray this faith is simply to undermine whatever competitive advantages have been gained over developments considered part of the suburban nightmare. This fact, of course, raises a host of other issues such as how to maximize the obvious benefits of a detailed plan while minimizing the necessity of making the kinds of promises that can only result in a sense of betrayal.

A community builder cannot predict with any certainty what precise course of action he will wish to take fifteen, or even five, years after he initiates a venture. Yet, as we have seen, to maximize immediate rates of sale, he must make specific commitments to buyers. A detailed plan or map and his reputation make these commitments believable. This situation, and the conflict inherent in it, suggests the following rule or formula for successful community building: find the smallest number of acres and the least number of promises which will still insure prospective purchasers that their class image and financial investment will be protected.

The formula is not an easy one to realize. For example, it seems apparent already that community builders probably have overestimated the market for multifamily housing. They will either have to develop the land zoned for this purpose at lower densities (and so reduce their potential return) or else hold it and wait. The latter decision is most likely. Yet it will produce "holes" of vacant land which may create rumors about future use. A more important problem of this sort concerns the builders' excess portrayal of industrial land use. Most buyers see industrial expansion (as long as it involves light industry and is separated from residences) as a reflection of the prosperity of the community and as a fiscal benfit. The present inability of a community builder to fulfill this aspect of the plan may suggest that other more important promises will not be kept.

Perhaps the crucial issue which could dramatize the community builders' dilemma as he seeks a balance between future promises and immediate realities is the potential introduction of lower-priced housing. If community builders find substantial demand for houses from $15,000 to $20,000 and for moderate rent apartments and try to serve it, their current residents may rise in righteous indignation. If analysis of their developments is valid, Rouse and Simon face especially difficult problems in this regard.

Rouse's cash flow and profit projections indicate the need to reach an annual absorption rate by the third or fourth year after the initiation of the community of 2,000 to 2,500 units per year. This necessity demands that he tap relatively low income markets ($12,000 to $16,000), as well as the middle and upper middle buyers sought by the Californians. Rouse recognizes the market dangers of mixing, so he intends to offer vastly different price ranges in different locations at the same time. But may not the strategy negate the advantage of protection which buyers seem to want? Rouse's planners argue that the very quality of the environment, particularly of the town center, will be their strong selling point. Yet not only will such an environment used in this manner cause higher costs early in the game, but the very diffusion may offset any advantages. It may be, however, that the low level of public services and amenities in some Maryland suburbs, as compared with developments in California, will give Columbia a needed advantage. In this sense the community will be worth study for, unlike any other, it proposes to sell objective environmental advantages more than class symbols.

At Reston, Simon does not at this point intend to reach a broad spectrum of wage earners. Instead he hopes to attract relatively high income people on the basis of aesthetics and the proximity of recreation and culture. As noted earlier, Simon's plan is dependent upon his ability to market attached houses at relatively high prices in a suburban location. If, at some later date, he feels it appropriate to shift to more conventional houses on moderate-sized lots for lower-income families, his early residents may consider it a violation of the promise that Reston is to be not only high status but high brow.

The Political Strategy of Community Building

The community builder's relation to state and local jurisdictions —as he seeks various commitments regarding zoning and subdivision regulations, road locations and interchanges, and the authority to create a district—contains the same type of potential dilemmas that are inherent in his relation to the consumer. The community builder wants to get these commitments while keeping as many as possible of his own options open. But if there appears to be any risk that a key requirement will not be granted or will be rescinded at a later date, the community builder will commit himself to certain objectives in order to get it. For example, Foster City represents a promise to the county and the state that the full operation will be carried out properly, that housing will be fairly expensive, that land will be set aside and held for industry, that park sites will be made available, that roads will be of sound quality and capacity, that utilities will be underground, etc. In return for these promises, the County has altered its master plan to permit a site for a regional shopping center, sufficient zoning for low- and high-rise apartments, and planned unit-zoning in some of the parcels. Similarly, the state granted Foster City the authority to issue tax-exempt bonds in whatever amount was required to finance site improvements, fill, and utilities.

What are the dangers in such a quid pro quo—dangers, it is possible to add, that community builders rarely face? First, by his promises to government, the community builder may freeze himself into positions which will be undesirable at some future date. For instance, if he finds the demand for industrial land low or nonexistent, he may wish to put land zoned for this purpose to some other use. But the county may hold that this would have an adverse fiscal effect on the area as a whole and refuse to rezone the land in question.

Second, there is some question as to the legal force of zoning over a long period. It is generally accepted that one legislature (or, in new communities, one Board of Supervisors) cannot bind its elected successor. Thus, it is conceivable that newly elected boards could try to change the zoning. The community builder, on his part, would argue that he had sizable investments based on prior zoning decisions. If actual physical work had been done on the parcel or parcels in question, there is little doubt that the developer would prevail. One cannot be so certain if the land was still untouched.

Third, the residents of the new community might try to form a city to include not only their homes but also the surrounding commercial sites and some undeveloped land. Such incorporation, including raw land, would vest zoning power in the new city rather than in the county. This eventuality is a possibility if in the residents' eyes the community builder appears to be breaking faith, especially by including lower-priced housing on smaller lots. In California, until recently incorporation could be effected by a majority vote of 500 residents. Now each county has a Local Agencies Formation Commission, LAFCO, which must approve the incorporation. A LAFCO potentially provides the builder with an additional form of protection against the dangers of incorporation.[2]

---

[2] LAFCO's and other proposed changes in California law may also inhibit community building in the future. All of the trends are toward more restrictions on the formation of special districts and the use of tax-exempt bonds to finance essentially private land-development ventures. If these restrictions become too onerous, or if the State says that tax-exempt bonds can be used only for publicly sponsored projects, an important source of low-cost, long-term money will have been eliminated.

Conclusion

As community building develops a market and political strategy, new kinds of problems arise, different from those which exist at the outset of the venture. This chapter has listed some of them. It is difficult to estimate how likely it is that these problems actually will come to pass or how serious they are likely to be. But that the new problems exist cannot be disputed. The issue is, then, whether community builders and their planners have faced up to this fact? It would seem that—based on interviews and observation—they have not.

Taxation as a theory of developmeent [handwritten annotation]

CHAPTER 8

Taxation

urban development [handwritten annotation]

COMMUNITY BUILDING aims at being a profit-making business, and part of the goal of any such business is to pay as little as possible of its profit in taxes and to delay those taxes it cannot avoid. This chapter examines those provisions of Federal tax law which bear upon community building. These laws are of great importance in influencing the decisions of *urban development* [handwritten annotation] community builders, including the initial decision to build or not to build, though it is difficult to offer much concrete evidence to support this contention.

Many rulings of the Internal Revenue Service rest on a judgment as to the "intent" of the tax payer. Thus, we made no attempt to ask community builders for their "true" intentions, as opposed to those given the IRS—that is to ask about the considerations which led them to signify one intent rather than another. Nevertheless, there is no doubt that builders have given much more careful consideration to tax issues than to the problem raised by their marketing and political strategies. In part this is because accountants and lawyers are much less sure than planners that *they can* predict the future with certainty; in part it is due to the fact that most community builders have had extensive experience either in real estate or oil ventures, two fields in which the opportunity to avoid or postpone income-tax payments on cash revenue is especially great. Finally, as was noted earlier, many community builders have substantial income from other sources and already are significant contributors to the Federal Treasury.

For such community builders there are three major considerations in judging the tax implications of a venture:

130

1. Which profits can be treated as capital gains rather than ordinary income?
2. Until such time as profits are realized, which costs can be deducted from other taxable income?
3. What are the opportunities to create and own income-producing improvements whose depreciation can be used to offset taxable income?

The Nature of a Capital Gain

There are three basic types of profit or income taxed by the Internal Revenue Service. The first is ordinary income to an individual. This consists of such things as salaries, consultant fees, interest on savings accounts, dividends, and income from personal investments. Since all community builders that have been studied in the Project operate through corporations, the regulations concerning personal income are not relevant.[1] The second type of income taxed by IRS is the ordinary income of a corporation. Prior to 1965, any such income over $25,000 per year was taxed at a flat rate of 52 per cent. Currently, it is being taxed at a rate of 48 per cent. To simplify the discussion, we will assume the corporate rate to be 50 per cent.

The third type of taxable income is income known as capital gains. The importance of the capital gain feature is that it carries a flat rate of 25 per cent of profits as opposed to the 50 per cent rate applied to ordinary corporate income. Thus, a corporation reduces its tax payment by 50 per cent to the degree to which it can have its profit treated as a gain on capital rather than as regular income.

There are two basic requirements for income to qualify as a capital gain. First, the profit must result from the sale of an asset, or from an instrument representing an asset (common stock or bonds), in a transaction occurring not less than six months after the purchase of the asset. Second, irrespective of

---

[1] T. Jack Foster and Sons is a partnership, but its tax incentives and disincentives are the same as for corporations.

the time from acquisition to disposition, the sale of such an asset or instrument must not be a part of the regular business of the corporation. In IRS parlance, the company cannot be a "dealer." Discussing the criteria for establishing whether a company is or is not a dealer, a standard reference work in the field, Montgomery's *Federal Taxes*, says:[2]

> If real property is held primarily for sale to customers it is not a capital asset . . .
> Whether a person is engaged in a 'trade or business' for tax purposes depends on the facts of each particular case, especially those facts as to frequency or continuity of the transactions indicating business status. In determining whether real property is held primarily for sale to customers in the ordinary course of business, certain well-recognized tests have been laid down: (1) continuity of sales and sales-related activities over a period of time; (2) frequency of sales as opposed to isolated transactions; (3) seller's activities such as improvements and advertisements to attract purchasers; (4) extent or substantiality of transactions; (5) reason for, and purchase and nature of, acquisition.

Judged by these five criteria, the historical land owner (such as Irvine and Newhall) is clearly not a dealer prior to his decision to become a community builder. He is not engaged in the business of developing and selling land. There has been neither "continuity" nor "frequency of sales." He has neither made intensive "improvements" nor advertised to attract customers. Occasional sales may have been made, but the transactions were not "substantial." The "purpose" and "nature" of the acquisition fifty to a hundred years ago was not to go into the real-estate development business. The land has been used for cattle grazing, growing crops, horse breeding, and so on. The fact that the owners of the land may be aware that its value as an area of urban development has long been greater than the value derived from its present use is, of course, irrelevant for tax purposes.

For a company owning a large parcel of land, the risk (potential cost) of being classified as a dealer is great. For example,

---

[2] *Montgomery's Federal Taxes*, 39th Edition (New York: Ronald Press, 1964), pp. 27–28.

10,000 acres purchased in 1900 might be on the company's books for $200,000 ($20 per acre). Its present value might be $30 million ($3,000 per acre). A sale of all the land to *one* buyer would be considered a capital gain. The tax would be 25 per cent of $29,800,000 or $7,450,000. On the other hand, if the company engages in planning, site improvements, and promotion, it will thereby become a dealer and be subject to a 50 per cent tax. In purely business terms, then, it would have to increase the value of the land by $14,900,000 (almost 50 per cent of the value before development), in addition to the costs incurred, to justify the effort of planning, improvement, and so forth.

Many large owners have chosen not to take this risk. For example, one corporation (the Lantain Corporation), formed by eight owners of 10,000 contiguous acres in the Santa Monica hills, did some planning and negotiated with the City of Los Angeles only so that the owners could sell almost one-third of the property to a developer and also assure themselves that traffic patterns and zoning would be satisfactory for the balance of their holding. Similarly, the owners of the 11,000-acre Albertson Ranch, immediately east of Janss/Conejo, sold the entire property (for over $30,000,000) to one buyer in 1962. Some owners, like Janss, have probably gone too far in preparing their lands for sale to maintain entirely a position as non-dealers.

It is possible for a real-estate developer to fall into both categories at the same time. Developing and selling the land to builders and individuals is "engaging in the business," and the profits are taxed at ordinary rates. But if other land is developed for investment, held for several years, and then sold, the profit on the *land* as well as the improvements can be treated as a capital gain. The tests here would be the length of time the property is held, the degree to which it actually yielded income, and the frequency of sales.

The likelihood that the sale of investment property will be ruled a capital gain is one reason for the great desire of community builders to develop and retain all the land they can for income-producing uses. For instance, a 100-acre site for a regional shopping center might be worth $10 million. Off-site improvements might cost $2 million. If the land cost were $2,000, the profit from the center when sold would be $7,998,000, which as ordinary income would be taxed at $3,999,000. However, if the center were developed and *held* for a few years, the tax would be only half, a saving of nearly $2 million. If the land and the improvements rise in value between the time of completion and the time of sale, the additional profit would also carry only a 25 per cent tax.

One of the most interesting and relevant examples is the Newhall Ranch, 44,000 acres owned by the The Newhall Land and Farming Company since 1875. Altogether, the Company owns a total of 150,000 acres in California. In 1948 it rejected a consultant's recommendation to sell 10,000 acres of the Ranch for $20 million and in 1963 it decided to create a new community. California Land Company will be the developer. Kerry Patterson, California Land's Executive Vice-President, described, during an interview, the corporate relationships and their tax implications.

California Land will buy land from The Newhall Land and Farming Company at market prices. It is purchasing 3,500 acres of useable ground for the first stage of development. It is intended that the Farming Company will itself develop such things as a golf course, commercial and rental houses—in other words, income property. California Land Company is a subsidiary of the White Investment Company. There is mutual family ownership in The Newhall Land and Farming Company and White Investment Company, but White Investment is not a subsidiary.

Thus it appears that the Newhalls will have the best of both worlds. The Farming Company will be able to sell land to California Land and pay only a 25 per cent tax. At the same time, land values will presumably rise as the result of planning and development. The ability to treat the profit from the sale as a capital gain rests on the fact that California Land is *not* a subsidiary of the Farming Company even though there is mutual ownership. A subsidiary company cannot be created by a historical land owner merely to avoid classification as a dealer.

Deduction of Early Costs

Community building is likely not to produce any profit for five or more years. The costs during these years include the land itself, off-site improvements (sewage disposal plant, water lines, major roads), on-site improvements (interior roads, water lines and sewer lines, grading), interest on borrowed capital, planning, administrative overhead, and promotion expenses. Clearly the cost of land and physical improvements are capital costs as opposed to expenses. In theory all costs should also be charged to capital cost of land, but their division among specific parcels could be subject for considerable debate.

In any case, the IRS will permit expenses to be deducted from current income, even in many instances in which the income is from a source unrelated to the expense. If community building produced immediate profits, the point would be academic. But since he usually experiences losses in early years, a community builder with other income will try to have the costs of the new community ruled an expense he can deduct from that other income. Let us suppose, for instance, that in the first year after starting a new community the taxable income from the other sources of such a company is $5 million. The tax on such ordinary corporate income would be 50 per cent or $2 million. Let us further postulate that the non-physical costs in the first year of the new community—planning, interest, property taxes, administrative overhead—are $2 million. If these costs can be treated as general expenses and deducted from current income, the tax liability can be reduced by $1 million.

It is certain that community builders handle at least part of their early expenditures in this way. This does not mean that the tax is permanently avoided. But it is delayed until profits are made in the new community. However, if any profits on the sale of land can be treated as capital gains, then there is a permanent advantage. The tax saved at the outset is at the rate of 50 per cent while the eventual tax paid is figured at the rate of 25 per cent. These relationships can be summarized as follows: When early costs are deductible from current income and are paid later as profits occur, the Federal government functions as a partner supplying capital with no return. When early costs are deducted from ordinary income and later profits are taxed at capital-gain rates, it is a contributor.

The Matter of Depreciation

The word "depreciation" generally means a reduction in value. In economic theory it refers to the real loss in usefulness or market value of a capital asset—a machine that wears out, for example, or becomes obsolete in a certain number of years. For income-tax purposes, however, depreciation is the amount which can be deducted from taxable profits *whether or not* an actual loss in use or market value has occurred. In point of fact, IRS laws and regulations permit deductions for the depreciation of improvements on income-producing real estate even when the market value of the property increases.

Let us assume a regional shopping center of 100 acres with a land value of $10 million. The improvements—such as buildings, parking areas, landscaping, on-site utilities—might cost $40 million. It is not possible to deduct any depreciation on the land. The amount that can be deducted on the improvements depends on their *economic* not their *physical* life. Their economic life might be twenty years. The annual deduction would then be one-twentieth of $40 million, or $2 million. This is called "straight-line" method of depreciation.

Another system, which is used more often, is called the "150 per cent" method. Here, one applies a constant rate of one and a half times the straight-line rate. In the example above, this would permit a deduction of $3,000,000 the first year. In the second year, again figuring on the basis of one and a half times the straight line rate, the deduction would amount to $2,775,000.

A third system can be used only when one is the original user of the property. It allows 200 per cent of the straight-line method. The possibility of this rate of depreciation is one of the reasons community builders want to develop and own income-producing property. Not only will their profit on the land be taxed as a capital gain (even if the owner is "dealing" in other types of land) but they get better depreciation treatment than if they bought already developed property.

Until 1964 the entire difference between the cost of improved real estate and its sale price was taxable at capital-gain rates, providing that the property was held more than six months and the owner was not a dealer. The accompanying set of figures showing the result under this regulation, of the sale of our mythical shopping center by a historical land owner (the original owner) after he had held it for two years.

Cost of 100 acres (actual value at time of development: $10,000,000)	$ 2,000
Cost of perimeter improvements	2,000,000
Cost of on-site improvements	40,000,000
Total cost	$42,002,000
Less 2 years depreciation using 200% method (20 year life)	7,600,000
Net book cost	$34,402,000
Sale price assuming 10% increase in value from date of completion	55,000,000
Less net book cost	34,402,000
Taxable profit	$20,598,000
Tax at 25% capital gain rate	$ 5,149,500

It is quite probable that the shopping center would not yield a net profit before taxes which equals or exceeds the depreciation of $7 million. An excess, however, is not lost to an owner who has other taxable income. Depreciation can be used to offset any income not merely the income from a specific venture or property. Therefore, the owner could deduct depreciation from income taxable at the rate of 50 per cent and later sell the property, paying a tax on the recovery of that depreciation plus any additional profit figured at the rate of only 25 per cent.

In 1964 the law was amended to say that to have all the difference between the value after depreciation and the original cost classified as a capital gain, one now must hold income-producing property for ten years before selling it.

A Special Example

Perhaps the influence of income-tax laws on the decisions of community builders is best illustrated by the situation of one company whose tax position is exactly the reverse of most community builders. Sunset International Petroleum Company entered real estate and community building in 1959, but it has continued to derive a significant share of its profit from oil production. The vagaries of oil-tax laws are too complicated and unnecessary to describe here. Suffice it to say that Sunset has a tax "shelter"—deductions from taxable income—far in excess of its current annual profits. Therefore, Sunset pays no tax on profits. In such a situation, in complete contrast to that of other community builders, matters of capial gain and depreciation are of no consequence.

Sunset views the conduct of business differently from other community builders for another reason. It is the only company whose stock is traded widely. One or two other community builders have some of their stock traded over the counter, but by and large they are family-held corporations with no public trading. Over 20,000 owners trade its six million shares on the American Stock Exchange. Sunset's ability to raise capital from financing institutions (which lend on mortgages or on general credit gained through the sale of bonds) is in part dependent upon the profits it shows and on the price of its stock. The latter obviously will vary directly with changes in profits.

Under these conditions, then, Sunset does not want to own investment property, for standard accounting practice would require it to take a straight-line depreciation. With no taxable income to be offset, this creates the adverse condition of reporting profits lower than they really are (if one assumes that the property does not in fact go down in value). This unusual set of circumstances does not mean that Sunset does not wish to secure zoning for apartments and commercial use whenever such arrangements would increase the value of their land. It does mean that the company sells or develops land only when it has made prior arrangements to sell the completed package.

Conclusion

This discussion of the Federal tax laws affecting new communities suggests that they pull in several directions. An owner of a piece of land which has risen in value (or is likely to rise) without any development on his part, and who also is not a dealer in land, risks losing a capital gains position (25 per cent of profits) for that of an ordinary income-tax payer (50 per cent of profits) if he chooses to undertake development. On the other hand, there are both capital-gain and depreciation advantages to development if one can retain significant amounts of income property. In addition, the principal investment disadvantage of a new community—its demand for cash outlays for several years—may be offset somewhat if the developer has other income from which his initial expenses in the new community can be deducted.

On balance, the tax advantages that accrue to community builders are not great (although some appear to have believed they would be substantial). In tax terms, an historical land owner who undertakes a new community without assurance that he can remain a non-dealer takes a large risk without the likelihood of high monetary returns.

CHAPTER 9

Community Building as a Business

THE THREE PRECEDING CHAPTERS have described and evaluated the political relations and marketing efforts of community builders, as well as some of the Federal tax ramifications of their activities. The main argument of the chapters was that community building is essentially a marketing and political strategy, and secondarily a tax strategy. It was our view that community builders often can be faulted for not giving serious consideration to important potential problems and conflicts in the areas of marketing and political relations, though their record is generally better in regard to tax issues.

But the practical operations of community builders are only a means to an end—a response to the urban-development critique that at the same time is meant to produce a reasonable rate of monetary return on capital and effort. Financial success is important to the builder not only for obvious reasons or because such success is a source of esteem, but also so that the initial new communities will serve as models for future endeavors. The purpose of this chapter is to describe the kind of business community building really is, even though such an analysis must be somewhat tentative since the process of community building is so young. The discussion focuses solely on business and financial issues. The issue of the possible social value of new communities will be considered in the next chapter.

As already indicated, most community builders have entered a type of business—land development—in which they have had little or no direct experience, despite the fact that many of them have considerable investments in improved and unimproved real property. Few of them have carefully examined the potential return, nor have they discriminated between re-

140

turn on investment and return on effort (also called skill, management, or entrepreneurial ability).

Return on investment is compensation for one's *money*. If one buys shares of stock in a company, his return comes in the form of dividends plus any gain he receives if he sells the stock for a sum higher than the one he paid. If the original price is higher than the resale price plus the dividends, there is a loss, or what is called a "negative return." Properly considered, return on investment is figured not only in terms of financial gain but also in terms of the *time* it took to realize the gain. In standard business and investment practice, then, the word, "return" is used to mean "annual rate of return." For example, if one buys shares of stock for $100 and sells them two years later for $110, the *annual* rate of return is less than five per cent.

As a rule, rate of return is directly related to the degree of risk involved—the higher the risk, the higher the potential return is likely to be. Thus, the investment in this country yielding the lowest rate of return is a United States Savings Bond or note, since repayment is guaranteed by the Federal government. (In countries with highly unstable governments and persistent monetary inflation, a similar situation probably does not exist.)

Return on *effort* is compensation for one's *time and skill*. While an investment of money requires some effort and knowledge, which theoretically should be separated from the return on the money itself, effort in itself implies a significant application of time and ability. A striking example of such effort is offered by the instance of James Rouse, who exercised great skill in such matters as land assembly, securing financial support, and political negotiation. Rouse's own investment of money in the new community of Columbia will be minimal in terms of the size of the venture. Thus, the return to Connecticut General, the major source of finances, will be calculated on the basis of invested capital, while the return to Rouse will be based largely on time and entrepreneurial skill. Admittedly, the latter is much more difficult to assess with precision.)

The central analytical question about a company or individual entering a field of business is as follows: *What is there about the inherent skill of the management and of the nature of the new field which seem likely to produce returns, as regards both effort and capital, that are greater than the returns available elsewhere for a similar commitment and risk?* This is the question this chapter will attempt to answer about the process of community building.

The Business of Land

SPECULATION

Before community building, there were two general methods of dealing with land development. The first of these is speculation.

A land speculator is a trader in land. He buys land with the intent of selling it at some later date for a sum sufficiently larger than the purchase price to pay his holding costs and deliver him a profit. By definition, a speculator does not perform any entrepreneurial function such as detailed planning, exercising a major effort to alter zoning, or installing improvements. His ability to secure satisfactory return (and to avoid loss) is dependent primarily on two factors: 1) his access to and understanding of information about the forces affecting land value, and 2) his holding costs.

Chapter 3 described some of the trends and governmental acts which have led to community building—a rising national income, population growth, development of freeways, water distribution, and so forth. A speculator must be aware of all such developments and of any changes which may increase or decrease the demand for land. In addition, he must be aware of the conditions of supply. For example, a speculator may be considering the purchase of a parcel of land which appears to be in the path of urban growth. However, he may have knowledge that several surrounding holdings are likely to come on the market in the next three years. If he has set for himself a holding period of three to five years, then this piece of information could prevent him from buying since it suggests the strong possibility of a potential glut of land offerings.

One could draw up an almost endless list of the facts and possibilities of which a speculator needs to be cognizant to make wise decisions or what can be called "educated guesses." He must be apprised not only of general demand for housing, stores, offices, or plants; he must also study the activities of builders and developers and their ability to raise capital. In short, the better and more complete his information, and the more intelligent his evaluation of it, the more accurate will be his judgment as to possible future prices.

The value of a rise in price is a function of the cost during the holding period. Part of this cost is property taxes, which are the same for any owner. More important is the cost of one's own capital, determined by the return one could get in other areas under similar effort and risk. For example, an investor can purchase a store with a long-term lease already signed by a large supermarket chain. His risk thus is negligible, and the annual return on his equity likely to be about seven per cent. (In addition, he will have certain tax advantages through depreciation. These were described in the previous chapter.) Land speculators seek higher returns, however, because their risks are considerably higher.

A speculator can increase his return by borrowing money at a cost lower than the expected return. There is a tremendous variation in the sources from which different types of speculators can borrow. Large corporations and extremely wealthy individuals can use their general credit to secure funds from financial institutions such as commercial banks and insurance companies at less than six per cent interest. Small companies and individuals with modest resources may have to turn to non-institutional or special sources whose interest rates normally exceed ten per cent. There are also wide variations in the size of a loan speculators are able to negotiate, and in the length of time they are allowed in which to repay it. In essence, speculation is a race between the cost of money and the increase in market value. Once the decision to speculate is made, the purchase price determined, and the loan terms established (either with the land owner or a lender), the speculator then simply waits. He does nothing to affect the future price.

His only activity is to decide the most propitious moment to sell.

Like the speculator, the land developer and merchant builder purchase land which they expect will rise in value. This expectation can be based in part on physical characteristics of the site—topography, trees, water courses, and soil conditions. More important is the probability that the land is in the path of urbanization and, further, that demand for property with similar characteristics is rising while the supply is diminishing. The merchant builder and land developer differ from the speculator in that they *add* value to the land through their own actions.

A successful land developer has accumulated a considerable body of knowledge and skills. He keeps track of land prices, rates of sale, and sizes of parcels in demand; he knows or can find out the type of zoning a local government is likely to assign in different areas. He is a capable negotiator with local officials and utility companies. He understands the qualities of sitework contractors and civil engineers and knows how to structure agreements with them to meet his needs. He has some sense of the market preferences of his prospective purchasers— small builders and individuals. He has sources of financing for himself and for his customers. He knows something about merchandising his product.

This skill and knowledge is by no means highly scientific. It is rarely codified. Occasionally it resides with one or two principals who have other business interests and only develop land sporadically. With other firms, several projects are always under way, and the principals rely in great part on second and third echelons of management.

The merchant builder possesses all of this skill and knowledge about land development. In addition, he knows how to mass produce and mass sell houses. Recognizing that great demand had been unleashed at the end of World War II by the mixture of FHA and VA programs, returning veterans, and rising incomes, aggressive men (many without any experience in the field) organized to capitalize on the opportunity. They concentrated on four operations: 1) finding land and financing its purchase, 2) establishing smooth working arrangements with FHA and VA, 3) negotiating with local authorities on zoning and utilities, and 4) creating a system of assembly-line production.

It was the last operation which really marked the emergence of the merchant builder as a new type. Mass production meant standardization and specialization of labor, instead of a situation in which a handful of men spent six months to a year on one house. The merchant builder created small crews, each of which handled a single aspect of the building process—framing, foundation forms, wallboard, siding, rough plumbing, finished plumbing, etc. Levitt, the master of such organization, formed crews which were paid by the unit rather than the hour. Simple but important power equipment—skill saws, pneumatic hammers, and staple guns—were introduced. Merchant builders subcontracted much of their work, but many of them exercised so much control over the contractors that these in effect were employees whose compensation depended upon performance.

Gradually also merchant builders changed the patterns of distribution concerning building products and materials. At first the demand that manufacturers bypass middlemen and accommodate products to the needs of the builder were met with replies about the need to protect the dealers. But soon manufacturers realized that the mass builders were by far the larger customers. By the end of the 1950's, almost every cabinet and appliance manufacturer sold directly to the builder at prices lower than those asked of dealers, and at specifications dictated by the builder to simplify field installation. Today, all but a few suppliers have direct lines of distribution to merchant builders.

As compared to the assembly lines producing automobiles or other products sold to a nationwide market, the methods of house production are still crude. Even so, during the sellers' market of the early postwar period, merchant builders made remarkable progress in holding down unit cost and simultaneously increasing production speed. In some of the larger operations, "starts" and "completions" were as high as 50 to 100 houses per week. Perhaps the most significant indication of the merchant builders' skill in production is the fact that from

1950 to 1960 most of them experienced little or no increase in the *per square foot* cost of their houses while their hourly cost for construction workers nearly doubled—and the quality of their product was vastly improved throughout.

During the 1950's, as builders refined their systems of production, accounting, financial management, and so forth, they began also to expand their interests. Without basic changes in technology (over which they had little control), the rate of improvement in production speed and efficiency they could achieve was diminishing. At the same time, land- and site-development costs continued to rise rapidly. Further, the era of a general housing shortage was coming to a close. Finally, most of the builders who had survived had created a sizable institution which needed to do a considerable amount of business just to support itself.

Thus, efforts were made to find more permanent sources of capital to finance land purchase and site work. Unlike the building of the house itself, no institutionalized financing existed for these operations. Housing production did not require major investments in plant or machinery. In addition, FHA-insured construction loans had been generous. Thus, builders could achieve sizable dollar volume with relatively little capital. A few builders sold stock or bonds to the general public. Others developed lines of credit with commercial banks. In California, savings and loan associations stepped in. Many builders were able to emulate larger American manufacturers and to plow back earnings into their businesses.

Recognizing that there were basic limitations on the volume achievable in any one location, builders began to engage in "multiple operations"—simultaneously developing several projects of varying price ranges in different geographical locations. With considerable success, they generally maintained the economies of scale that previously had resulted from high volume at one site. But a multiple operation meant greater attention to such matters as systems of cost and quality control, accounting procedures, and logistics of material delivery. In short, it demanded a refinement of management techniques and the development of a cadre of second-line managers.

The most profound change that took place, however, was the builders' growing attention to marketing procedures. At first this meant only an improved method of merchandising. Model homes were elaborately furnished and landscaped; sales offices with displays were erected; advertising agencies and advertising managers were employed; full- rather than part-time salesmen were hired. Then the product itself became a matter of serious concern. Architects were consulted; systems of information retrieval, concerning the wants of buyers and prospects, were developed; the concept of the product itself was widened to include not merely the house but its immediate environment. Landscaping was installed, community centers and swimming pools were built, street patterns were varied. Recently, emphasis has been put upon open or common space and underground utilities.

This brief discourse on the merchant builder is a description, in effect, of the creation of an industry. By some standards, its behavior is crude. Moreover, not all merchant builders fit the pattern described here. But more and more the field is being dominated by firms that see themselves as permanent institutions which have acquired certain skills, contacts, relationships (with banks, subcontractors, suppliers, local officials, and consumers), experience, and capital that cannot easily be duplicated by new entrants. Few people would now think of becoming automobile manufacturers, for the present ones are just too far ahead. Homebuilding is not likely ever to reach this stage. Regional differences in climate and tradition, technology, and many other factors mitigate against such a tight oligopoly. Nonetheless, the current general trend (especially strong in California) for merchant builders to eliminate the land developer as a middle man—except in the creation of resort, retirement, or very high priced housing—has every probability of continuing.

It is not an over-all increase in demand which has characterized the housing industry during the last ten years. Rather it is the fact that an increasing share of this demand is being served by merchant builders. This trend can be broken only for one of two reasons. First, a severe recession or depression (or war) might so limit demand that few firms could keep even the shell of their organization intact. Second, a new kind of entity could enter the field with skills and resources that would result in cost reductions or qualitative improvements (or both) not otherwise attainable by either merchant builders or commercial and industrial developers.

The Place of the Community Builder

The community builder has entered the field of land development as a mixture of the speculator and the developer. There are three main reasons why an individual or a firm enters a new field: 1) the firms already in it may be making high profits; 2) the new entrant may be able to perform the same functions as these other firms with greater efficiency; or 3) there may be untapped demand for a type of product or products which the present firms are unwilling or unable to offer to consumers. The following discussion shall measure community building against each of these criteria.

PROFIT TRENDS

It is very difficult to get accurate data on rates of return in real estate. When a corporation trades its stock publicly, it is required to publish periodic profit and loss statements and balance sheets. But because most real-estate operators are individuals or closed corporations, such public reporting is rarely available. Thus, analysis of this subject is necessarily impressionistic.

Nonetheless, between 1945 and the late 1950's or early 1960's it is relatively clear that substantial profits were made by a great many individuals and companies speculating in and developing land, especially in California. In the past four or five years, though, opportunities for fairly rapid and high returns have diminished. In part, this has occurred as a result of the operations of merchant builders, who successively merged the processes of speculation, land development, and homebuilding. As merchant builders and their counterparts, commercial and industrial developers, found institutional sources of capital, the possibility of high returns to nonprofessional investors also diminished. At the same time, there was during this period the inevitable overestimation of future prices on the part of speculators.

It also appears that in general the profits of the professional firms themselves went down in the last few years (although there are surely many exceptions to this trend). There is general consensus within the industry that profit margins and rates of return on capital were lower from 1960 to 1965 than in the preceding decade and that those companies which had maintained or improved their position had done so as a result of exceptional management skill.

It is clear therefore that community builders have not entered a general field characterized by rising returns. Significantly, at no time in interviews or discussions did any community builder assert that this was the reason he undertook his venture.

RELATIVE EFFICIENCY

The second possible reason for entering a new field is a belief that one can carry out the functions of existing firms more effectively than they do. In part, the success of merchant builders rests on the ability to increase efficiency, which they did by improving techniques for the production and merchandising of houses. Since community builders do not as a rule build houses nor sell them for merchant builders, these are not areas in which they would assert any significant management superiority. Like professional developers of shopping centers and industrial parks, community builders contract for construction. Through observation and experience, they may acquire skill approximately equal to such professionals, but there is no likelihood they will be able to surpass them in the ability to develop and manage income property.

Community builders do install site improvements such as sewage disposal plants, water mains, and major roads. Some even complete the sitework for each lot—grading, streets, sidewalks, utility lines—so that the area is ready for house construction. However, they tend to handle such activities in much the same manner as do land developers or merchant builders. Consulting engineers design the improvements and then put them out to be bid upon by contractors. Given their lack of experience, community builders will be fortunate not to be at a disadvantage in site work as compared to other developers. After contracts are let, delays and higher costs can be incurred because of unforeseen soil conditions and weather, factors which are extremely difficult to predict.[1] Merchant builders and land developers have learned that adverse effects of unpredictable occurrences can be minimized only by constant and competent field supervision. Community builders may not have a comparable competence. Finally, as to the size of the site: although a 500- or perhaps a 1,000-acre tract may offer economies of scale in site work over one of 50 or 100 acres, it is very doubtful that any economies are to be accrued from land over 1,000 acres.

It was pointed out earlier that community builders *do* have marked success in matters of zoning, which under certain conditions can raise land values considerably. This relative advantage, a function primarily of the size of the community builder's holding and of the fact that the land is under the jurisdiction of a county rather than a city government, works to the benefit of the community builder. Its value, however, is limited (at least in California) by the relative permissiveness of most local governments and by the lack of foreseeable demand for "higher" land uses (apartments, and industrial and commercial uses).

A most important factor in the operation of a real-estate venture, especially a long-term one, is the *cost* of money. Community building might be characterized as a race between the cost of carrying charges (principally in the form of interest) and the rise in land values. The same can be said about speculation, but for a community builder the cost of money is greater because he not only holds land but also adds substantial improvements to it. One community builder described the operations of his business as follows:

---

[1] Site-work contracts generally provide that the contractor is not responsible for any such developments.

Basically we are storing money in land. Community building is a high risk and potentially a high return form of capital growth investment. It is not an attractive vehicle for speculation because of the heavy front money requirements and the extensive management commitments, nor is it attractive as a manufacturing operation because of the difficulty of matching cash inflows with cash outflows to produce satisfactory current returns.

To illustrate the nature of community building as a business, a financial model of a hypothetical new community called Eastvale was prepared. The data, or inputs, do not represent those from any of the projects studied. In deciding what figures and relationships to use, every effort was made to decide in favor of the community builder.[2] For example, the model assumes an annual sale rate of over 2,000 housing units starting with the fourth year after land purchase. To date, no new community has achieved an annual sale rate even of 1,000 units.

TABLE 1A

Annual Cash Movements of Eastvale without Financing and Normal Land Sale Prices

(*All Figures Rounded to Nearest Thousand*)

Year	Development Expense (cash out)	Cash Proceeds (cash in)	Annual Net Cash Move- ment	Cumulative Net Cash Movement
1	19,419	—	–19,419	–19,419
2	192	—	–192	–19,612
3	920	—	–920	–20,532
4	283	1,275	992	–19,540
5	18,552	3,580	–14,972	–34,512
6	382	6,380	5,998	–28,515
7	631	8,150	7,519	–20,996
8	330	8,150	7,819	–13,177
9	500	8,150	7,650	– 5,527
10	24,382	8,150	–16,232	–21,759
11	2,519	10,020	7,501	–14,258
12	2,445	11,890	9,445	– 4,813
13	2,471	11,890	7,519	4,706
14	2,286	9,740	7,454	12,159
15	2,264	13,746	11,482	23,641
Total	77,480	101,121	23,641	

Rate of Return = 6.4%

---

[2] A complete discussion of the model appears in Appendix II.

152 | *Community Building as a Business*

TABLE 1B

Annual Cash Movements of Eastvale with 4 Per Cent Financing of
75 Per Cent of Total Cost and Normal Land Sales Prices
*(All Loans Are for Number of Years Left in Project; All
Figures Rounded to Nearest Thousand)*

Year	Debt Service	Total Cash Out	New Loans	Total Cash In	Annual Net Cash-Move-ment	Cumulative Net Cash Movement
1	—	19,419	14,565	14,565	−4,855	− 4,855
2	1,623	1,815	144	144	−1,671	− 6,526
3	1,598	2,518	690	690	−1,828	− 8,354
4	1,641	1,925	213	1,488	− 437	− 8,791
5	1,762	20,315	13,914	17,494	−2,820	−11,611
6	3,896	4,279	287	6,666	2,389	− 9,223
7	3,825	4,457	474	8,624	4,167	− 5,056
8	3,791	4,121	248	8,398	4,277	− 779
9	3,719	4,219	375	8,525	4,306	3,526
10	3,682	28,064	18,287	26,437	−1,628	1,899
11	8,399	10,918	1,890	11,910	992	2,891
12	8,733	11,179	1,834	13,724	2,545	5,436
13	8,915	11,286	1,778	13,668	2,382	7,818
14	7,779	10,066	1,715	11,455	1,389	9,208
15	6,843	9,107	0	13,746	4,639	13,846
Total	66,207	143,687	56,419	157,533	13,846	

Rate of Return = 11.2%

Tables 1A and 1B demonstrate the flow of costs and revenues as Eastvale progresses. Even a casual reading of the tables reveals that large sums of money flow out in the early years and that revenues do not begin until considerably later.

In addition to this general picture of cash flow, a computer model was developed which permits calculating the rate of return for a new community, as well as the effect upon the rate of variations in costs, financing terms, sales rates, prices, and so forth. Using the data shown in Tables 1A and 1B, first a rate of return on invested capital was calculated, assuming no use of borrowed funds. Then projected sales prices of land were raised and lowered by 10 per cent each way and a 75-per cent financing of total cost at both 4- and 6-per cent interest was assumed.

The figures of a 75-per cent loan and a 6- and 4-per cent interest rate were chosen for the following reasons: Seventy five per cent is the maximum percentage provided in the Federal loan-insurance proposal (see Chapter 10), and a figure no lender is likely to top. (Rouse apparently has secured a much higher loan, a subject discussed later in this chapter.) A 6-per cent interest rate is the lowest conceivable rate given by a private lender, and also the rate provided in the Federal program which insures loans to private lenders. The 4-per cent interest rate was chosen because it is about the cost the government would charge if it made direct loans or engaged in community building itself. Also, the interest cost on special district bonds approaches this figure, as evidenced by the Estero District's (Foster) last bond sale at an average yield of about 4.6 per cent. The entire analysis is based on a concept called "present worth" or "discounting," which assumes that money spent early or received early is worth more than funds spent or received later.

The results of the calculations are shown in Table 2. The first striking result concerns the rate of return under conditions of no financing and at the "normal" sales price. It is only 6.4 per cent, a very low return for what the community builder quoted above characterized as a "high-risk" venture. With 75-per cent financing of the cost, at a 6-per cent interest rate, the return on equity is increased to 7.4 per cent, an increase in the rate of return of 15.6 per cent. The same loan at a 4-per cent interest causes a more dramatic rise. The rate of return becomes 11.2 per cent, or a percentage increase of almost 60 per cent.

The simple rule or formula which can be derived from these findings is that large loans can significantly improve the rate of return, particularly when *there is a marked difference between the rate of return without borrowing and the interest rate at which money is borrowed.*

Table 2 also indicates the effects of 10-per cent variations, up and down, in the sales price of the land. Without financing, a 10-per cent increase in sales prices raises the rate of return from 6.4 to 8.7 per cent, an increase of 35 per cent. A 10-per

Table 2

Eastvale: Variations in Rate of Return as a Result of Varied Sales Prices and Financing

	No Financing	Financing: 75 Per Cent of Cost 6 Per Cent Interest	Financing: 75 Per Cent of Cost 4 Per Cent Interest
Sales price 10 per cent down	4.0	Loss	4.0
Normal sales price	6.4	7.4	11.2
Sales price 10 per cent up	8.7	13.2	16.4

cent decrease has the same effect in the other direction. When financing is introduced, the changes resulting from differing sales prices are even more dramatic. The large variations on rate of return shown in Table 2 as a result of only a 10-per cent variation in sale prices indicate that community building is truly a high-risk undertaking. In Eastvale a 10-per cent reduction in sale prices, when the project is financed with loans covering 75 per cent of the cost at a 6-per cent interest rate results in a loss. Even with a loan at 4 per cent and sales prices 10 per cent *higher*, the return on equity before taxes is only 16.4 per cent.

Thus, unless the absorption rate was seriously underestimated, or sales prices that are much lower than they would be in actuality were projected, or costs were vastly overstated, the rate of return in community building is low in light of the risks it involves. Even an average manufacturing company expects a return of 20 per cent or more before taxes.

UNTAPPED DEMAND

This analysis leads directly to the third possible reason for entering a business field—the belief that there is significant potential demand which existing firms are unwilling or unable to tap. If this is so for new communities, then community builders may be able to achieve sales rates and prices sufficiently high to produce satisfactory rates of return. This, in fact, is much the position that community builders have taken in explaining their objectives. They have based their decision to develop new communities largely on the assumption that the application of professional planning to a large amount of land will create a product far superior to available alternatives and that will be viewed as such by the consumer—the alternatives (and competition) being the new house offered by a merchant builder or an existing house offered for resale.

However, is this a fair expectation? Chapter 7 considered the impact of planning on the consumer, and saw that to him "planning" was quite different from what it means to a professional planner. More important, when planning is applied to land at the edge of the metropolis, especially in California, the "planning" the consumer sees may offset only partially the locational disadvantage of such a site. As one California community builder said: "Community building is valid if it brings land to the market faster than would otherwise have been the case." This study judges that the benefits of such acceleration are more than offset by the costs, especially early outlays for utilities and roads, some of which would be borne by the general process of urbanization if the land holder simply waited.

From this point of view and responding solely to the goal of achieving a reasonable rate of return (let alone a maximum one), the best policy for a large landholder might well be to do nothing with his land until it is marketable to professional developers by virtue of increasing urbanization. Planning would still be required, since few professional developers would buy more than a fraction of the land at one time, and would mean some control over such activities as sizes and alignments of roads and utility lines. Until his land was marketable, however, the owner's only possible activity (for income-tax considerations) might be to try and secure zoning for potential income-producing property and to retain such land for future development. One conclusion of this book is that this is precisely what a great many incipient community builders will do as time goes on.

Columbia: A Potential Exception

One reason it is so difficult for California community builders to get any competitive edge in their developments is that high-quality public services already exist in most urbanizing areas, and a vast amount of land already adjoins good roads and utility systems. These conditions do not exist, at least to the same extent, in all other areas of the United States. It is in part for this reason that James Rouse's prospects at Columbia may be somewhat different from those outlined in the preceding section.

It is worth reviewing Rouse's situation. The differences between the conditions at Columbia and those in California are as follows:

1. There were few large parcels near Washington or Baltimore under single ownership.
2. The quality of local public services—sewer, water, county roads, libraries, police and fire protection, schools, etc.—was generally much lower than in California.
3. Special districts with authority to issue tax exempt bonds were not being used by land developers in the Baltimore-Washington area.
4. Baltimore and Washington were growing rapidly toward each other, creating the possibility that a project could tap *both* markets.
5. While most California counties were moving toward more flexible and permissive zoning, elected officials in Howard County had committed themselves to half acre lots—to stave off rapid urbanization.
6. The state highway program was much further advanced in California than in Maryland.

Despite the fragmentation of land ownership, Rouse, through careful control and negotiation, acquired (at what seems a reasonable price) over 15,000 acres of land with sufficient contiguity to be treated as an entity. He secured a loan amounting to almost 100 per cent of the purchase costs (nearly $25 million), and has now put the loan on a more permanent basis and found financing for the installation of physical improvement. With a project requiring a net cash outlay in excess of $40 million over the first two-year period (for land purchasing, planning, utility arrangements, and zoning) and the first five years of actual development, Rouse will receive half the profits and have invested less than $1 million.

In California, while planning no doubt has played some part in securing desired zoning, it has not been of overriding importance (reflected in the Janss Company's loose and fluid approach in Conejo and in its success with Ventura County). In Howard County, though, planning was essential to secure zoning changes. Had Rouse been required to adhere to the half-acre lot pattern, the maximum number of housing units available to him—30,000—would have been significantly reduced by the fact that he would have used a portion of the land for recreation, schools, industry, shopping, etc., not to mention the land covered by creeks, steep grades, and rock outcroppings. Instead, by submitting a fairly detailed plan, Rouse received permission to use smaller lots and also build some apartments, so that he can devote large amounts of land to non-residential uses and still have the full 30,000 units.

Extremely important for the possibility of Rouse's future success is the apparent commitment Howard County has made to him on commercial zoning. As of now the county seems to have taken the following position: "We shall zone about 100 acres for your town center, which will be the regional shopping center for 300,000 people"—thereby "giving" to Rouse a population and area more than twice that of Columbia. If this is the arrangement that has been worked out, Rouse will have a near monopoly on the most valuable kind of land use. Californians seek such preemption, but most cities and counties in California take the view that the market should be the prime determinant of commercial use. Thus, Janss/Conejo has 100 acres zoned for a regional center, but it is doubtful that Ventura County will refuse similar zoning for the 11,000-acre Albertson ranch less than three miles away.

Like other community builders, Rouse intends to offer housing (by merchant builders) at prices similar to those offered at locations closer to the center of the metropolis. He hopes that the high quality of Columbia's physical facilities and services will more than offset the extra distance. If commuters buy fast enough in the first few years, industry is sure to follow. Moreover, the growth of Washington and Baltimore insure that eventually Columbia will not be a fringe location. The central question is how long this growth will take and how much Rouse can do to affect its rate.

This question is another way of asking whether Columbia will be successful. By virtue of his own perserverance and skill as negotiator, manager, and salesman (to financiers and political officials) and, with the help of an accomplished staff, Rouse has acquired vast acreage and gotten favorable zoning and utility conditions. This promises him the probability of a competitive edge over other landowners and developers, since he will be able to offer merchant builders and others desirable features not to be had at other sites. It is doubtful that even the most experienced land developer or merchant builder could have exercised the ability or the imagination to duplicate Rouse's effort. But whether Rouse might have applied himself and his resources to other enterprises which would net a greater financial return is not known. Since the funds for Columbia will be supplied almost entirely by lenders, Rouse need only achieve a rate of return slightly higher than the interest rate he is paying to realize for himself a very high rate of return on his own investment. This might not produce a yield commensurate with the risk[3] and the effort, but even moderate financial success may be satisfactory to Rouse if Columbia fulfills its non-monetary objectives as he sees them.

Conclusion

This chapter has dealt solely with community building as a business. It has maintained that, as a business, the risks of such a venture are high. Community builders, who have been

---

[3] Rouse risks not only his time and money but, to the degree that he must provide at least a reasonable return to his lenders, his reputation as well.

less skeptical than the authors of the validity of long-run prediction, do not as a rule hold this view. In addition, the evidence to date concerning the basic market assumptions on which the whole process of community building is premised (evidence discussed in Chapter 7), suggests that these assumptions are either false or at least vastly exaggerated. In the light of the risks involved and the apparent invalidity of its market assumptions, community building thus seems unlikely to result in monetary returns commensurate with its risks.[4]

None of this is to say that the non-monetary gains of new communities might not themselves be high. If this were to be true, then a case could be made for governmental intervention to improve the financial climate of community development. The next chapter addresses itself to this question.

---

[4] This analysis has not discriminated between a community builder who purchases land specifically to build a new community and an historical land owner such as Irvine Company or the Janss Corporation. An evaluation has been based on the assumption that land is recently purchased, which is true for most new communities in the United States.

An historical land owner can choose among several alternatives. He can do nothing; he can sell his land in bulk; he can do minimum planning and development and sell off in large blocks; he can become a community builder. The decision is affected by many factors such as the number of family members involved, the financial positions of the respective owners, the skills and interests of respective owners, and the tax implications of each alternative. Such a situation is too complex and subjective to evaluate in terms of a monetary rate of return.

CHAPTER 10

New Communities and
Public Policy

IN 1963 the California Housing report proposed a two-fold program to help initiate new communities—state loans to community builders or direct purchase of land by the state. In 1964 and 1965[1] the Johnson Administration asked Congress for authorization to make loans either to private sponsors or to the states for the same purpose. None of these measures was enacted, but all were based on the thesis that underlay the Community Development Project—that there are serious problems in American society which can be attacked by a new method of developing land at the fringe of metropolitan areas. The thesis held further that large areas of such fringe land should be planned and developed by a single entity.

This is the belief shared by the authors when they undertook this project to try and devise one or more demonstrations which would act as a catalyst in spurring changes in public and private policies. Now, research and reflection has produced quite the contrary view—that community building, even with public aid or under public sponsorship, can do little to solve the serious problems confronting American society. This sharp about-face is due in part to a changed conception of what constitutes a "serious problem," and in part to a changed view of the type of action appropriate for government to take. This chapter, beginning with a review of the powers available to the various levels of government, takes a detailed look at the arguments for and against government support of new communities.

---

[1] The same proposal was rejected by Congress again in 1966.

The Powers of Government

LOCAL GOVERNMENT

The primary point of interaction between a community builder and government occurs at the local level, principally the county. If a local master plan of the area exists, this plan determines the uses to which the developer may put his land—residential, commercial, industrial, and so forth. If a master plan does not exist, then the local government makes its determination on the basis of a plan submitted by the developer. Beyond this, zoning ordinances specify what is permitted within each category in regard to such items as lot sizes, building heights, the portion of a site which can be covered by a building, and the ratios of on and off street parking. Subdivision regulations further specify street and sidewalk widths, requirements for street and sidewalk construction, maximum slopes, and so on.

As a rule, community builders submit their own plans. To secure flexibility not possible under regular zoning ordinances and subdivision regulations, they try to create planned-community ordinances, or use those already in existence.

The other important power of local government is to grant the right to establish a special district with authority to issue tax-exempt bonds. Normally, election to the newly created district board is determined by assessed valuation of property. Since community builders own a great deal of land and expect to develop and retain income property, they should be able to maintain control almost indefinitely.

It seems clear that local government might take certain kinds of demands in return for its cooperation with community builders. But as the previous discussion has shown, by and large no such demands have been made, except of course that community builders fulfill their plans.

THE STATE

All of the powers of a local government are granted by the state which created it. This relationship is not analogous to the relationship between the states and the Federal government, for the latter was also a creation of the states. The United States Constitution˙sets forth the rules of the state-national government compact. It provides, for example, that police power (except in special and proscribed circumstances) rests with the states. Zoning and subdivision regulations are based, in turn, on the police power granted to units of local government.

As noted earlier, the Local Agencies Formation Commissions (LAFCO's) were created by the California legislature in 1964 as the result of the proliferation of local governments. Small cities, especially special districts, had been severely criticized for their inefficiency, the low turnout in district elections, and their interference with regional decision-making. In some states, such as Minnesota, such criticism has caused the state government to create a commission to pass on proposals for the creation of new local governments.

Thus a state can facilitate or inhibit community building by altering the power of local government and the requirements leading to their formation. It could aid community builders by making the creation of small cities more difficult or even impossible, thereby removing the threat of early incorporation (which would give residents control of zoning). But it could inhibit the process by banning the creation of special districts or limiting their formation to taxing areas created and administered by city- or county-elected officials. This policy would restrict or eliminate the use of tax-exempt bonds to finance utilities and other improvements in new communities. It appears that this is precisely the policy which Maryland and Howard County followed in refusing to authorize any kind of taxing district for Columbia.

A state has also the power to react more directly to community building. It could adopt legislation removing local control over new communities and placing it instead in a special commission which would review the plans of applicants and decide which community builders are entitled to special dispensations. Of course a state also can program public works, such as freeways, water distribution, and institutions of higher learning so as to facilitate development.

A state can go even further and use its own credit and its power of eminent domain to acquire large parcels of land and finance both acquisition and site development. As in redevelopment, the state government could sell the improved sites to private corporations, with contractual restrictions upon their use. (While there is some doubt about the constitutionality of a state using the power of eminent domain to acquire raw land from one private owner and transfer it eventually to another, the courts are likely in most cases to accept the judgment of the legislature that this is a legitimate public purpose.) The ultimate state powers of condemnation and credit could be granted to a development corporation initiated by profit seeking sponsors but containing representatives of the state, the county, surrounding municipalities, and so on.

Almost any action by a state to change the nature of new communities, or to create more or less of them, would require legislation. Such legislation is quite conceivable since it would be based on the historic state powers of establishing local governments, using eminent domain and state credit for public purposes, and building certain kinds of public facilities.

THE FEDERAL GOVERNMENT

The Federal government has few programs which have as their direct purpose the creation of a specific pattern of urban development. Nonetheless, a great many Federal actions influence this development.

Programs enacted to affect physical development are administered chiefly by the Housing and Home Finance Agency (HHFA) and the Bureau of Public Roads. HHFA does not deal directly with the consumer, nor does it construct or determine the location of a public facility. What it does is to provide loans, loan guarantees or insurance, and grants to junior governments and private institutions. Its programs include: low interest-rate loans to local public agencies for facilities (sewage disposal, water supply, mass transit); matching grants to states, cities, and counties for planning; loans and grants to local public agencies to construct low-rent public housing; loans and grants to local public agencies for clearance and rehabilitation of slums (urban renewal); insurance to private lenders who provide loans at (or near) market interest to home buyers or to builders of rental housing (FHA); and insurance for loans made by the Treasury through the Federal National Mortgage Association to non-profit or limited dividend corporations for the construction or rehabilitation of housing for middle-income families (earning from about $4,000 to $8,000). In addition, the Bureau of Public Roads makes matching grants (as high as 90 per cent) to the states for interstate highways.

By and large these programs have had their effect only since World War II. In the great debate about their influence upon the character and pattern of urban growth, they have, at the very least, encouraged the trend towards lower densities in all land uses and the decentralization of industry and commerce. Also, they have helped to harness the housing demand pent up until after World War II and fed since then by rising incomes. Despite this, it still would be difficult for the government to administer such programs to affect dramatic changes in the density or placement of new development because the programs function indirectly—they aid only the action of other parties.

Thus Federal programs do not have a strong, direct effect on community building. Some merchant builders sell homes with FHA or VA loans, but were the government to attach any requirements which the builders saw as onerous, they could shift to conventional loan sources without drastically altering their sales rates. Public-facility loans and planning grants have not been used because the developments are private projects, nor has the middle-income housing program been used even when the development could be considered eligible.

All of this is simply to say that as a practical matter the Federal government does not currently have much of a carrot with which to influence community building one way or the other. Yet, it was the Federal government (with no outside influence seeking its intervention) which first decided to take some action. So far HHFA[2] has been unsuccessful in its support of the proposals it derived from the California Housing Report (to provide loans to both public and private sponsors for land acquisition and site improvements in new communities), but it is expected that the Administration will continue to press for them. The key provisions in the bill it sponsored were as follows:

1. FHA would insure loans for land purchase and development.
2. The Federal National Mortgage Association would be authorized to purchase such loans. (Private lenders might not be willing to hold such loans even with FHA insurance).
3. Insured loans could provide as much as 50 per cent of the cost of the land and 90 per cent of the cost of site improvements, but could not exceed 75 per cent of the value as determined by the FHA Commissioner.
4. The maximum loan would be $25 million.
5. The Commissioner should assure himself that the planning would be made "effective."
6. The Commissioner should encourage housing for low- and moderate-income families.

As indicated in the last chapter, the provision for such long-term, low interest-rate (6 per cent) loans to a community builder could have a significant impact on the return he receives on his capital. In addition, such loans would enable many firms to undertake a new community for which sufficient funds might not otherwise be available, from any source at any cost.

---

[2] Since the completion of this book, the HHFA has become the Department of Housing and Urban Development. Congress enacted Title X (Housing and Urban Development Act of 1965) enabling the Department through the FHA to insure loans for land development. In 1966, Title X was expanded to embrace new communities. Insured loans under Title X have a maturity of up to seven years.

Virtues and Threats

The general consensus on new communities has been that they can contribute greatly to the public good but that they require 1) financial aid, with certain strings attached, from the Federal government and 2) some added regulation by state and local government.

It has already been noted that junior governments have the necessary power to provide such regulation if they care to do so. But the question is to what purpose such power should be put at any level of government.

Since the Johnson Administration is a strong supporter of a loan program to aid new communities, it is not surprising that one can find articulate justification for the program in the statements of the government's representatives in HHFA, even though these ideas did not originate primarily from within HHFA but represent the thinking of many experts. Its most comprehensive defense is to be found in a speech given at the University of Illinois by Dr. Robert Weaver, the director of HHFA. Because of its comprehensiveness, Dr. Weaver's speech (now published in book form)[3] serves as a useful basis for discussion. We wish to emphasize here that we respect Dr. Weaver as a dedicated public servant, and to state that he is presenting a position developed only after consultation with a great many city planners and developers. It is this position, and not Dr. Weaver as an individual, with which the following discussion is meant to take issue.

SCATTERATION, EFFICIENCY, AND THE JOURNEY TO WORK

Many contend that new communities will decrease the journey to work as well as to other activities. It is argued that this would save public costs for transportation, utility lines, school busing, etc. In addition, the residents of new communities

---

[3] Robert C. Weaver, *Urbanization in the Middle and Late 1960's*; The Lorado Taft Lecture (Evanston: University of Illinois, March 18, 1964).

would have the advantage of being close to a variety of facilities and services. As Weaver put it in his speech: "More rational development of the surburban areas would minimize transportation needs and utility line extensions. And, too, the development of satellite communities affording employment opportunities, as well as educational, recreational and commercial facilities, would serve the same purpose."

How are these advantages to come about? First, the supporters of new communities argue, such developments would contain higher densities than those of conventional suburbia. But the projected density for most new communities is 3 to 3.5 dwelling units per acre, which hardly indicates great compaction. Indeed, it would require density of at least triple this figure to make any major difference in utility or transportation needs than now exists. Since the 3 to 3.5 figure appears to reflect the mutual desires of house consumers, retailers, and industry, it is unlikely that a governmental agency could establish significantly higher densities, except by adopting extremely restrictive measures.

The supporters of new communities also argue that the communities offer greater opportunities for local employment, recreation, culture, and commercial activities than do other types of development. However, while such opportunities are brought about in new communities with a marginally higher degree of speed than normally, it is nonetheless the case that the development of surburban housing on fragmented parcels has consistently been followed by the appearance of industry, recreation, and commerce. In fact, one aspect of the urban-development critique, and a cause also of federally financed urban renewal, is the accurate contention that central cities are losing their industry and commerce. The point is, stores and plants *are* relocating in the suburbs. Moreover, there is little a community builder could do to attract such facilities to his particular project, even with the aid of any of the powers now available to government.

In Great Britain, the publicly initiated new towns do serve as industrial sites, but only because there are a host of formal and informal controls regulating industrial location. Theoretically a

national policy to regulate industrial settlement could be enacted in the United States (in combination with a new community, new towns, or even a new metropolis policy), but
this is far more drastic action than the advocates of new
communities propose or, apparently, desire. Without such an
effort, however, new communities will follow the regular pattern of development. Residents will arrive first, and the growth
of local commerce and industry will follow. Moreover, as in
Janss/Conejo most new residents will be traveling further to
work, and to many other places, than they did before they
moved. It is true that some recreation facilities are built very
much earlier in new communities than they would be in other
developments, but, as noted, the lakes, golf courses, and parks
are more for providing symbolic investment protection for the
residents than great opportunities for their enjoyment.

Finally, it has been argued that new communities would
reduce utility extensions and transportation needs because the
communities would develop more rapidly than do areas under
fragmented ownership. At the moment, there is little evidence
that this is so, but here government action *could* make some
difference. State and local governments could give zoning and
other advantages to selected new communities (by constructing a freeway to them, for example, or a university campus
within them). If Federal aids of this kind were passed along to
the consumer in the form of lower prices, better houses, or more
amenities, sales would obviously be spurred.

Still, if densities are not likely to be raised, the *total* amount
of land consumed by a new development, whether it is in a
new community or not, will remain the same. Thus, those who
are staggered by the fact that "the process of urbanization con-
sumes a million acres a year,"[4] can find no consolation in the
advent of new communities, with or without government aid/
or control.

But what about the prevention of "scatteration" which leaves
holes of undeveloped parcels of land all over the place? Isn't
this a beneficial consequence of new communities? Wouldn't

---

[4] President Johnson's message to Congress, March 12, 1965.

it reduce the cost of public facilities and services and increase services? In the short run it might, but no reliable evidence has yet turned up which projects savings of sufficient magnitude to warrant the necessary rationing of land use and selection of some land owners for such gigantic favors.

Since the prevention of scatteration or, as it sometimes is called, sprawl, is emphasized so strongly by the supporters of new communities, it might be well to consider in more detail what the terms mean, what evils come with them, and what new communities might do about them. Harvey and Clark give the following definition:

Sprawl, measured as a moment of time, is composed of areas of essentially urban character at the urban fringe but which are scattered or strung out, or surrounded by, or adjacent to underdeveloped sites or agricultural uses. A sprawled area has a heterogeneous pattern, with an overall density less than that found in mature compact segments of the city. Sprawl areas are less dense than would be found if the areas developed for housing would be developed with discipline exercised in the assembling of jig-saw puzzles by adding pieces from the bottom up.[5]

The authors go on to cite the causes of sprawl, among them tax laws, zoning regulations, mortgage policies, fragmented ownership of land, and the character of land developers. Clearly community building, at is has been discussed here, eliminates some of these factors. But to what extent are such defects critical? Harvey and Clark go on to identify two fundamental aspects of sprawl which most commentators have failed to recognize.

The first is time. Sprawl usually occurs at the fringe of a rapidly growing area. It is costly to the degree to which capital must be used to install sewer and water lines, roads, and so forth earlier than if development had proceeded in a more compact manner. However, since the area is growing rapidly, the gaps will be filled in quickly and the extra costs will be minimal. As Harvey and Clark argue: "A static or very short-

---

[5] Robert O. Harvey, and W. A. V. Clark, "The Nature and Economics of Urban Sprawl," *Land Economics*, XLI, 1 (February 1965), pp. 1–9. Harvey is an economist, Clark a geographer.

run view on urban development permits an exaggeration of development cost per unit, which cost may in fact be modest on a unit basis once the development is viewed as a complete entity."[6]

Even more important is the second issue they raise—of who bears the extra cost, if any, of sprawl. Freeways are usually installed without regard to the specific character of urban development. Thus the capital cost of freeways is probably unaffected by sprawl. Sprawl may increase driving time and cost, but these burdens are borne by the resident not society. Again, most scattered projects (at least in California) must pay for the cost of longer runs for sewer and water mains. But here too, it is the resident—not society—who pays the price.

However, in some cases this situation does not obtain. Electricity and gas, for instance, are supplied to almost any site, and the costs of their distribution are reflected in *general* rates. Thus, all users share the burden of capital outlay. In such circumstances, a change in laws and regulations is required so that the specific users pay the cost of their locational choice without subsidy from society as a whole.

It cannot be said that new communities necessarily reduce the extra costs which supposedly come from sprawl or scatteration, for usually communities leapfrog open land and so require extensions of utility lines. From society's viewpoint, however, their value is that these burdens accrue to the land itself, in the form of lower receipts to the land owner or higher costs to the new user. In any event, if one keeps in mind the concept of time, sprawl does not seem to result in additional economic cost of great magnitude. The same can be said about esthetics, for the unsightliness of scattered development is only temporary.[7] If one is concerned not just with scatteration

---

[6] Harvey and Clark, *op. cit.*

[7] There is a growing body of opinion questioning the supposed ill effects of sprawl. Indeed economist Jack Lessinger sees positive benefits in it:

"In general we hypothesize that scatter suits an economy where growth and technological change predominate. Compaction may suit a stabilized economy, without inequalities in the distribution of income, seeking optimization of its resources." Lessinger, *AIP Journal*, XXVIII, 3 (August 1962).

but also with the visual quality of developed suburbia, one really is objecting to the taste of America's middle class. We find it difficult to believe that market-oriented new communities, aided by Federal loans, will drastically alter such esthetic values.

Supporters of new communities are on fairly strong grounds when they cite greater open space as a likely consequence of new communities. To be more precise one might say that when community builders dedicate open land to a public agency or a home-owners association, the land is likely to remain largely undeveloped for a long time. When ownership is fragmented and open space is desired, the local government must purchase the land to prevent it from being used. If the government waits until surrounding land is developed, then the price it must pay becomes very high.

With community builders, however, the cost of the open land is added onto the price of the developed land. Thus, in effect new communities offer consumers the opportunity to pay for open space and amenities as part of their house purchase. Since there is no evidence in California that consumers will buy these benefits by trading off smaller lots, they necessarily must pay in some other fashion—a longer journey to work, higher prices, smaller houses, or a combination thereof. In any case, it should be noted that whatever the consumers decide, more permanent open space within a new community will mean more scatteration, an evil supposedly avoided by community building.

HOUSING MIX

The most persistent argument for aid to, and control of, community building is that it does not provide housing for lower income families under present circumstances. It is argued that large enclaves of middle- and upper-middle-class residents are in themselves inequitable and otherwise undesirable. This was the principal reason for the program proposed in the California Housing Report. Weaver puts the case simply when he writes: "There can be, and there should be, an economic mix in the population of new communities in a democracy."

But this represents a vast oversimplification of the situation. We have already seen that the very thing buyers in new communities hope to avoid is the inclusion of lower-income families. One can recognize this without approving of it. Further, it also appears that lower-income families are improving their residential status precisely by occupying the housing left vacant by the more affluent, and that most of the housing is closer to blue-collar employment than are the new communities. There is, no doubt, some amount of subsidy which would induce lower-income families to move to new communities, and also to get higher-income residents to tolerate this. But such subsidies would certainly have to be far larger and more direct than a loan to the developer.

An increasing amount of economic separation seems more or less inevitable then. However, there are certain problems which might follow from this development that can, to an extent, be controlled. The first is the possibility that the wealthier members of society may use their spatial homogeneity to create local governments which would insulate them from contributing to the costs of the services provided for the less advantaged in the country's urban centers. However, the more taxes collected at the state and Federal levels and then returned to local governments on the basis of population and/or need, the less meaning tax enclaves have. The country increasingly is operating in just such a manner. In California almost half the cost of primary and secondary education is borne by the state. The newly passed bill providing Federal aid to education further contributes to the trend. We shall return to this point again.

The other serious problem that stems from separation on the basis of income is that it is also likely to mean racial separation. Yet how much can be done about this through any policy of controlling or aiding privately sponsored new communities? In regard to housing policy, it seems crucially important that a single, simple principle ought to be followed wherever possible. To improve the housing of those with low incomes, one should give direct aid and let the recipients make their own choice as to where they want to live. In 1965 Congress enacted a program of rental supplements which points in this direction. Direct loans at low interest rates and grants for home ownership would also be appropriate.[8]

Most other attempts to use more devious, although perhaps politically more palatable, devices have largely failed to get assistance to those who most needed it. Further, despite the good intentions of the proponents of Federal aid to new communities, there is not much chance, for the reasons already outlined, that many families with low incomes would become residents of these developments. Once the loans were made, the FHA would be strongly interested in the financial security of the project. What would an administrator do when confronted with the quite plausible assertion that the market for low-priced houses is not big enough to support a new community and that, indeed, the few such houses that could be sold might severely decrease total sales?

SITE PLANNING, DESIGN, AND INNOVATION

Weaver, along with many other supporters of new communities, believes that in addition to attacking the broad social questions of public costs and the relationship of classes and races, new communities also will offer more efficient use of specific sites, more creative design, and even outright innovation. Commenting on the possibilities of efficient site planning, Weaver writes:

> Even if the cost of acreage increases, the price of a developed site to the homebuyer need not advance to the same degree. Indeed, good planning can produce improved lots at a lower cost to the home owner or renter. This has been, and can be, accomplished by greater clustering of dwelling uints and inclusion of town houses and apartments on a portion of the available land in the development areas, so that the amount of land that has to be graded and improved is reduced. Streets and utility lines are shortened, cost of construction per dwelling unit is sometimes reduced at the same time that the

---

[8] State of California 4 per cent loans to veterans are an example of such a form of direct subsidy. But such loans should be made on the basis of need rather than military service.

number of housing units in the site is increased. In addition such site planning requires less bulldozing of trees, greater preservation of other scenic attributes, and wider possibilities of open space.[9]

Most of this argument is fallacious insofar as it implies that all these accomplishments are more likely to come about in new communities than in an amalgamation of subdivisions. The key word in the argument is one which has gained an almost mystical quality in the lexicon of land development—"clustering." Clustering means the concentration of buildings on less land than would otherwise be used. The land that is thereby saved can be put to some public (or at least pleasing) use—a lake, golf course, a park—or it can merely be left untouched.

In some parts of the United States, local jurisdictions have restricted housing development to very large lots—one-half to four acres. Under such conditions, land can be better used in terms of economy, esthetics, and, ultimately, market response if houses are clustered on smaller lots (7,000 to 15,000 square feet). This is precisely what Rouse has proposed for Columbia. Figure 1, taken from Columbia's brochure, illustrates the principle.

Clustering can be accomplished even when ownership is fragmented. The kind of land ordinarily left unused is a mixture of hills, valley streams, rock outcroppings, etc. In other words, it is the land most difficult to develop and therefore least valuable in money terms. A county could make a master plan identifying such areas for open space and recreation, and then purchase them. The price would be nominal, especially if the land is bought before there is much surrounding development. Minimum lot sizes for the remaining land could then be reduced. The net effect would be exactly the same as clustering.

Government purchase of land for open space would raise the value of the land not purchased, but this is also what happens with a community builder. If a county felt that the benefits from such expenditures did not accrue to all its citizens, it could establish an assessment on the area affected. As

[9] Weaver, *op. cit.*

residents and other land consumers took title, they would pay for the amenities, which again is what happens in a new community. The higher tax on the land, due to its increased value as well as the county's special assessment, would increase the probability of its sale for development. Holdouts might still occur, producing greater scatteration than in a new community. Since scatteration is not an unmitigated evil, this is not a serious drawback. Because land ownership usually is not concentrated, and because its assembly is extremely difficult, government should devise methods for reaching its objectives with or without single ownership.

A different kind of clustering occurs when the maximum lot is already as small as 6,000 square feet (the case in most parts of California). In this situation, land can be freed for other uses, or higher densities can be obtained, only by attaching houses. This results in what is now called the "suburban town house," referred to in the discussion of Reston. Weaver seems to be promoting such a concept when he says: "This type of land planning runs counter to the tradition of a free standing house in the 'country' surrounded by a large lot; however, where it has been well done, the consumer response has been favorable."

Of course people differ on their definition of what is "well done," but most suburban town house developments have not been favorably received by buyers. (As noted, the early evidence at Reston does not in market terms justify Simon's decision to base his whole plan on this concept.) On the other hand, it can be argued that suburban town houses offer some people a physical arrangement not otherwise attainable and that sales will improve as time goes on. But the key point here is that whatever the demand for the type of house now or in the future, its development does *not* depend upon large scale ownership. In 1964, over 100 town-house projects were started in Orange County, California, none of which were in a new community.

A third way to produce clustering is to build more apartments on any given piece of land than might otherwise have been erected and then to transfer the land saved (assuming constant over-all density) to open space or public use. Again, there is nothing intrinsic to new communities that would prevent this from happening elsewhere. If a county wants a higher density of apartments, it can achieve this by zoning regulations. It then can either purchase the unused land for open space or require that developers hold it, as a part of a quid pro quo for the apartments.

In predicting that new communities will bring a tide of new creative design and innovation, its supporters are on even more tenuous grounds. In the process of development, the community builder necessarily becomes a land manager trying to maximize the value of unused holdings. His essential job is to conserve, to make sure that nothing goes on the land which will have a harmful effect in the future. This is hardly a climate from which unusual physical forms are likely to emerge. In fact, one may well find community builders rejecting novel proposals of merchant builders because of the uncertain effect they will have on the value of the land. Simon, who is trying to make of Reston a "laboratory" for one new approach to suburban design, is an exception, who only proves the rule.

Problems of Federal Aid

New communities *do* offer some improvements in the physical environment and some choices which consumers have not often had. A new community offers a consumer the opportunity of paying either through a longer commuting time or a higher price for a house (or both) for parks, lakes, golf courses, and underground utilities. Whether he makes this choice for esthetic or status or investment reasons or to use the recreational facilities, is not relevant.

However, it is one thing to recognize a few product improvements and another to argue that public funds, through tax-exempt bonds or direct Federal aid, should be used to aid in their creation. To whom would the benefits of such aid flow but either to present land owners or to the middle and upper income families who avail themselves of the opportunity to live in a new community? Thus, such aid would represent government's commitment to confer minor benefits upon the least needy families.

Moreover, a program of loans to community builders is fraught with paradoxes and pitfalls. In the first place, the developers most likely to apply for help are those with the least desirable and riskiest sites. An entrepreneur convinced he can do well without Federal aid is not apt to subject himself to the myriad of controls that such aid would no doubt entail. Since the state of the art of market analysis is so low and since the terms of a loan can so markedly affect the rate of return, FHA would almost be bound to set conditions to try and insure success.

Again, what would constitute an acceptable rate of return on a loan and how is it to be calculated? These are questions FHA has not had to face because in all its dealings it could rely on past market transactions. But no history of the sales of 10,000-acre holdings is available to help determine questions of market value in the case of new communities. A vicious circle would be created. The value of land and of improvements can only be determined by sophisticated investment analysis which depends on one's ability to predict the capital costs and also demand, a highly unscientific affair. If the loan is favorable enough, almost any project will succeed because it will be able to withstand high early costs and slow sales. The effect of such favorable terms would be to increase artificially the value of the land.

Still another difficulty of providing community builders with the Federal loans concerns the methods FHA would use to see that a builder's original plan is carried out. A FHA loan normally is based on a study of detailed plans and specifications, which the builder promises to follow. But is it possible or even desirable that the same method be adopted in regard to a fifteen-year project? How detailed can the plan of such a project be? To what degree can a builder adhere to it? With as much as $25 million committed to a single project, FHA in fact would have to permit changes to protect its insurance. Yet these changes might well be in conflict with the very purposes of the original program.

There is no need to go on endlessly describing the difficult decisions facing the government and the financial uncertainties involved in a program of such loans. Our case must rest on the claim that the risks are high and the potential benefits minimal.

Public Sponsorship

The second part of the new-communities section of the 1965 Housing Bill is a program of low interest-rate loans to state land-development agencies. This program is designed to achieve the same results as the program of direct loans to builders, with the difference that here the benefits of increases in land value at least would go to the government. But in so far as the results are the same, the program, in our opinion, is essentially no more valid.

There is one condition, however, under which public sponsorship might be useful: if it were made part of a program of research and demonstration. The building and development industry does not have firms large enough to engage in serious technological research. On the other hand, basic science and technology probably hold much that could be applied to make great improvements in local transportation, communication, air temperature control, illumination, more flexible houses, etc. The government would be spending its money wisely if it used it to ferret out these applications and then sought to test them in a development like a new community. Obviously, this is not the sort of research or the sort of risks a private sponsor would be willing to undertake.

A second kind of experimental program might involve racial integration. Very little is known about Negro demand for housing, but it is possible that Negroes are extremely reluctant to buy new housing. They may fear difficulties in the buying process itself or hostility from the other residents, and they may want to be assured that there will be enough Negroes in the project for a reasonable social life. (Such fears are probably strongest in working and lower middle class Negroes.) A public or publicly funded non-profit sponsor could be committed to maximizing opportunities in such a way that 10 to 30 per cent of the residents would be Negro. The demonstration of what it would take to make such a project viable could provide sorely needed information on how to open up the suburbs to Negroes as they rise financially.

It cannot be stressed too strongly that such programs should be public efforts directed to the provision of *information*, and not the first step in a statewide or national program of public land ownership. They should be part of an over-all effort at the state and Federal level to improve the flow of information to local agencies, public and private.

General Framework

In none of the foregoing do we mean to imply that there are not urgent urban problems with which the country must grapple—among them, water and air pollution, transportation deficiencies, inadequate housing for the poor, fiscal inequities, mal-distribution of water and power, and mal-apportioned legislatures. That there are such problems is only too obvious. But that the best way to alleviate them is through "long range" physical planning, if this means precise guidelines and concommitant constraints to "achieve the plan," is very much open to question. As political scientist Charles Linbloom has put it:

Although such an approach [long range planning] can be described, it cannot be practiced except for relatively simple problems and even then only in a somewhat modified form. It assumes intellectual capacities and sources of information that men simply do not possess and it is even more absurd as an approach to policy when the time and money that can be allocated to a policy problem is limited, as is always the case.[10]

Present urban problems can be dealt with far more effectively through changes in institutions and laws which seek to remove obstacles to equity and choice. For instance, the judicial decisions on racial segregation in public facilities (beginning

---

[10] Charles Linbloom, "The Science of Muddling Through," *Public Administration Review*, XIX, 2 (1959), p. 80.

with Brown vs. the Board of Education, in 1954) and on legislative apportionment (beginning with Baker vs. Carr, in 1963), are having a profound and salutary effect on the life of the country. The same will be true of the voting rights measure which Congress enacted in 1965. All these actions enable deprived citizens to have more freedom in using public facilities and in influencing their government.

The so-called Heller Plan,[11] which consists of sharing a certain portion of Federal revenues with the states, similarly addresses itself to a serious institutional problem—that the nature of our economy and our tax laws makes it very difficult for the states to raise funds commensurate with their responsibilities. The Federal government already shares its taxes through programs of grants and loans to state and local authorities. The states in turn share their revenues through general subventions and grants for specified use. Under the Heller plan, tax sharing would be increased. Further, the senior government would rebate funds, but the junior government would decide how to spend them.

Even without tax sharing, a local electorate might appropriate funds for certain needs through regional or metropolitan authorities (though in many cases the creation of such entities would involve the crossing of state lines). Two examples of such local action, by dealing with problems of transportation and pollution respectively, are the New York Port Authority and the Los Angeles Air Pollution Control District. Federal and state action to create regional governments might well constitute the removal of a further institutional barrier to constructive progress.

As mentioned earlier, the absence of large producers or consumers in the areas of housing and public facilities makes it difficult to apply basic science and technology to these concerns. The Federal government, recognizing a similar circumstance in agriculture three decades ago, undertook then an ambitious

---

[11] Walter Heller, formerly Chairman of the Council of Economic Advisors to Presidents Kennedy and Johnson, made this proposal in 1964. Johnson has rejected the idea, but in 1965 several Governors strongly endorsed it.

program to improve knowledge and disseminate information through direct research and agricultural extension. A Federal program of research and development to improve both the quality and quantity of schools, hospitals, transportation, libraries, and housing would be equally desirable.

Another useful program would be to give low income families greater purchasing power in the form of direct income supplements to be used for the rental or purchase of housing. Such a program would allow these families much greater latitude in deciding where to live and in what sort of housing.

The basic point of all these potential programs is that they increase the ability of private and governmental institutions to offer individuals an opportunity to make their *own* choices, whether with dollars or votes. This approach might be called "instrumentalism." Judicial decisions, legislative or administrative controls, subsidies, dissemination of informaton, restructuring governmental jurisdiction, and research may all improve "instruments" which help to keep a society pluralistic and open. Insofar as this is what the proponents of "planning" mean by the term, it is highly desirable. What is not desirable is "long-run" decision-making for its own sake.

Of course, there are "instrumental" actions which are bound to have effects for decades. (The San Francisco rapid transit system is one example.) In such instances, one must try to take into account all these effects while, at the same time, recognizing that predictions have a limited certainty. The aim should be always to avoid rigid determinations about life twenty years in the future. This book has criticized planning for new communities because it tried to chart such a course. It should in general be doing quite the opposite—measuring the restrictions a current act or decision may place on one's freedom to choose among alternatives at a later date. This is the approach that should underlie all public policy. Its object is not fixed forms *or* inaction but programs which maximize the ability of policy makers and their constituents to choose among a set of varied courses.

The brief of this book has been with the arbitrary and purposeful preclusion of choice which seems to underlie so much of the advocacy of new towns, new communities, and other efforts to map specifically future settlement patterns. British economist Peter Self, an ardent supporter of new towns, succinctly articulates this point of view when he writes:

The New Town approach does not deny the value of mobility, but tries to distinguish between its less and more essential aspects, and to stress that there are after all other values besides mobility and maximization of choice in jobs, homes and friends.

Maximized choice is not necessarily an optimized choice, and recognition of community values, of aesthetic patterns and of over-all economic efficiency, do all in their different ways stress the point that atomistic individualism should be restrained by other perceptions.

Unlike Self, the authors believe that "optimized choice" *is* "maximum choice"—that what is needed from government are laws and programs which allow every individual to do, and be, what he will. There is little potential for new towns or new communities to contribute to this goal. The money and the energy which might be committed to expanding opportunity for the poor, the young, the aged, and the sick should not be diverted to real-estate ventures, no matter how noble the motives of their sponsors. Most of the people in this country who really need help—for whom the urban complex is least effective—live in the central cities. It is to these people in their present environment, primarily, that attention and money should be directed.

Appendixes

New Community Developments, 1964

New Communities	Location	Acres	Housing Units	Projected Population	Building by End of 1964
Arizona					
Goodyear Farms	W. of Phoenix	13,000		50,000	X
Lake Havasu City	Lake Havasu	13,000		50,000	X
Tucson Green Valley	S. of Tucson	10,000		25,000	X
New Tucson	E. of Tucson	16,500		100,000	X
Sun City	N.W. of Phoenix	14,000		75,000	
California					
El Dorado Hills	Sacramento County	9,800	20,000	75,000	X
Sunset	Sacramento County	12,000	31,000		X
San Marin	Marin County	2,000	5,000	15,000	X
Foster City	San Mateo	2,700	11,000		X
Rossmoor Leisure World	Contra Costa County	2,100	10,000		X
Conejo Village	Ventura County	11,000		87,000	X
Albertson Ranch	Ventura, L.A. Counties	11,500		100,000	
Diamond Bar	Los Angeles County	8,000	20,000	75,000	X
Porter Ranch	Los Angeles County	4,100	12,000	43,000	
Mountain Park	Los Angeles County	7,150		60,000	
Crummer Ranch	Los Angeles County	6,300		50,000	
Irvine Ranch	Orange County	93,000		300,000	X
Huntington Beach	Orange County	1,000		10,000	
Rossmoor Leisure World	Orange County	2,465	18,000	30,000	X
Leguna Niguel	Orange County	7,100		90,000	X
San Carlos	San Diego County	5,000	9,000	35,000	X
Ranch Bernardo	San Diego County	5,400	11,000	33,000	X
California City	Santa Rosa				X
Mission Viejo	Orange County	7,000			
Rancho California	San Diego County	87,000			
University City	San Diego County	13,000			
Colorado					
Columbine	Denver	7,000			X
Colorado City	S. of Pueblo	5,000		30,000	X
Pikes Peak Park	Colorado Springs	4,300		30,000	
Village East	E. of Denver	1,000		10,000	

New Community Developments, 1964 (Continued)

New Communities	Location	Acres	Housing Units	Projected Population	Building by End of 1964
Delaware					
Mill Creek	N. of Wilmington	1,300	5,000	13,000	X
Florida					
Miami Lakes	N. of Miami	3,000	6,000	25,000	X
Canaveral Princeton	SW. of Cape Kennedy	2,500		43,000	
Port Charlotte	N. of Punta Gorda	92,700		100,000	
Palm Beach Lakes	W. of Palm Beach	7,000	25,000	70,000	X
Lehigh Acres	E. of Fort Myers	60,000		80,000	X
Deltona	SW of Daytona	15,000	41,000	75,000	X
Georgia					
Chapell Hill	Atlanta	1,100	2,900	12,000	X
Illinois					
Elk Grove	N. of Chicago	3,000	10,000	35,000	X
Oak Brook	W. of Chicago	3,600		25,000	X
Weston	W. of Chicago	4,700		50,000	
Kentucky					
Oxmoor	W. of Louisville	1,000		15,000	
Louisiana					
New Orleans East	E. of New Orleans	32,000		175,000	X
Maryland					
Columbia	Howard County	14,100	29,000	110,000	X
Crofton	Ann Arundel County	1,400	3,500	13,000	X
Joppatown	N. of Baltimore	1,300	3,000	10,000	X
Northampton	Prince Georges County	2,200	8,000	25,000	X
Massachusetts					
New Seabury	S.E. Cape Cod	3,000	3,750	16,000	X
New Mexico					
Paradise Hills	W. of Albuquerque	8,500		60,000	X
New York					
Sterling Forest	Orange County	20,500			
Oregon					
Somerset West	W. of Portland	6,600	12,000	40,000	
Texas					
Clear Lake City	S. of Houston	15,000	40,000	150,000	X
Horizon City	E. of El Paso	65,000		100,000	X
Virginia					
Reston	Fairfax County	6,750	24,885	75,000	X

APPENDIX II

A Note on the Economics of Community Building

by Ted Dienstfrey

Often what is meant by the statement that a community builder is engaged in a profitable business is simply the idea that this investor will receive more money than he spends.[2] What is missing from such a notion of profitability is an appreciation of the number of years this investor must wait before he gets his return. Ignoring this time spread between money going out and money coming in, not only makes it impossible to compute a rate of return, but also tends to hide the economic risks of such a project.

This paper is based on the assumption that discussions of the profitability of community building ought to be discussions of the average annual rate of return of these investments.[3] What follows is a description of one method of computing a rate of return for community building. Since this computation implies a model which defines the community building process, the model will also be described.

Often, if one can conceive of a model of a process, it is relatively easy to translate this model into a usable computer program. To the

---

[1] This research was sponsored by the Community Development Project which was established by a Ford Foundation grant to the Center for Planning and Development Research at the University of California, Berkeley. I am indebted to Edward Eichler, Project Director, and John Dyckman, Center Director.

The main findings of the project are reported in this book, and in Carl Werthman, Jerry Mandel, and Ted Dienstfrey, *Planning and the Purchase Decision*, Preprint Number 10, Center for Planning and Development Research, University of California, Berkeley, California, July, 1965.

[2] For the purpose of the studies done in connection with this project, a community builder is defined as "an owner of a large, continuous parcel of land (2500 acres or more) who aims at applying the 'best' known techniques of planning to develop industrial, commercial, residential, and public facilities, as well as amenities not normally found in new suburban developments." See Preface.

[3] A rate of return may be viewed as that interest rate which a bank would have to pay an investor in order to make a savings account in that bank as profitable as the contemplated investment in community building.

187

degree that the model represents the actual development process, one can use the associated computer program to test the profitability of various development plans. The results of testing the economic implications of a prototypical community building investment with an existing computer program will be reported.

The first conceptual problem in analyzing community building involves isolating the community building investment from other types of real estate investments. The easiest way to accomplish this isolation of community building investments is to assume that all land developed in the community building venture is sold. Even though most community builders intend to retain ownership of the commercial properties involved with community building, it is not unreasonable to place a sales price on these rental properties. Establishing a sales price is no more hypothetical than establishing a rental income stream. If one expects low initial rents to be followed by higher future rents, and if this expectation is reasonable, one can establish a sales price or present worth price that reflects this maturing of property.

The assumption that land is sold has several advantages. First, it brings to light the "business" of community building. The community builder is in business because he can bring some increment of value to raw land either by the fact that he is offering a unique product, in this case supposedly a new and better environment that has some market value, or by the fact that he can develop land more efficiently than his competitors. Second, it forces the analyst to try to measure the actual net increment in land value that the community builder is delivering.

The assumption of land sales, called here the "forced" sale of land, results in what some might call a limitation of the model. The model because of this forced sale ignores the tax-shelter advantages of depreciating investments in real estate improvements. However, ignoring income taxes and the difference between the before tax and after tax returns at this point means simply that one is trying to compute just what profits might need sheltering.

This decision on the income-tax problem dispenses with annual statements of profit and loss. This means that two of the most difficult issues of accounting associated with annual statements, first, the allocation of cost to parts of the total project and, second, the estimation of the value of the yet undeveloped and unsold land, can also be ignored. Both of these problems are basically accounting issues. By continually raising the book value of the unsold land and/or maneuvering the allocation of cost, one can, by the stroke of an accountant's pen, hide for many years the true economic nature of a project. Although a particularly skillful accountant can delay the realization of true worth of an investment, he cannot change the value of the total worth of the propect. By means of a complicated set of weighting, a series of annual accounting figures can be summed to give a total project average. Since this model is an exercise in investment alternatives and not accounting alternatives, nothing is lost and simplicity is gained by looking at the total life span of the project instead of a series of individual accounting years associated with annual statements.

The variables left for the model to handle lend themselves to an economic analysis revolving around the concepts of cash-flow table. The economic effects of alternative physical development plans are easily observed in the particular dash-flow table generated by a particular plan.

Having decided on the conception of a model, in this case an annual cash-flow analysis, one is left with the physical computer problem of how much flexibility one wants to program for. The degree of flexibility is related to the skill of the programmer and the level of detail in data which is expected. Since the model is now programmed to include certain types of unit-development data which no developer has currently assembled, the model at present is slightly "over-programmed."

The sales variables the model accepts are yearly sales rates for up to eight types of land with each land type having a separate, variable sales price. Built into the program is a terms of sale condition which assumes that each year's sale will generate a cash proceeds in the year of sale equal to 50 per cent of the sale and the remainder appearing as cash proceeds in the following year.

The program accepts five types of costs: 1) project costs such as land cost and major utilities which are entered for specific years; 2) a cost of sales that is some percentage of total sales; 3) a unit development cost which varies with the amount of land sold in each of the eight land categories and has a one-year lead time; 4) special costs that occur after some percentage of the total amount of single family land is sold; and 5) real estate taxes that vary with the rate of land sold.[4]

There is no doubt that one could have a problem which comes closer to simulating the actual process of development; that is, a simulated audit program. However, such a program would not only require more data than the project at present has been able to collect, but considering the hypothetical nature of all planning data, would also result in much greater complexity in data handling with no accompanying gain in accuracy. At any rate, at this point cash flow analysis is taken as the basis for the model.

---

[4] Ted Dienstfrey, *Financial Viability of Large Land Developments*, Unpublished Thesis for the Master in City Planning, Department of City and Regional Planning, University of California, Berkeley, California, January, 1966.

The computer program first prints out in a series of suitable formats the various input variables and then prepares an annual cash-flow table before financing (Appendix Table 1). From the cash-flow table, one can easily see the special peculiarities of a community builder's investment. It is inherent in building a community that the builder must not only lay out large sums of money for major utility systems, primary roads, and, sometimes, freeway interchanges, but that the builder is, in effect, acting as a land banker. These characteristics of the investment show up in a cash-flow table as large, annual, negative cash flows in the first few years of a project.

Taking the annual net cash flow (line 11 on Table 1) the program computes an average annual internal rate of return using the following equation:

$$\sum_{j=1, N} \frac{F_j}{(1+R)^j} = 0$$

where F = net cash flow or net cash movement
j = year
R = rate of return

Basically the rate-of-return equation is a special case of the more familiar present-worth equation.

$$\sum_{j=1, N} \frac{F_j}{(1+R)^j} = \text{Net Present Worth}$$

In the present-worth equation one assumes some discount factor, "R," and using the annual net cash flows, solves for the net present worth. In the rate-of-return equation, one searches for that discount factor which sets the net present worth equal to zero.

An example might help to clarify the relationship between these two equations. Suppose that one invests $10,000 for two years at which time one will receive a total return of $12,100. What is the net present worth discounted at 5, 10, and 15 per cent?

At 5%, $\text{NPW} = \dfrac{-10.0}{(1+.05)^0} + \dfrac{12.1}{(1+.05)^2}$

$\text{NPW} = .97$ thousand

At 10%, $\text{NPW} = \dfrac{-10.0}{(1+.10)^0} + \dfrac{12.1}{(1+.10)^2}$

$\text{NPW} = 0.0$

At 15%, $\text{NPW} = \dfrac{-10.0}{(1+.15)^0} + \dfrac{12.1}{(1+.15)^2}$

$\text{NPW} = -.86$ thousand

It was stated that the discount factor which sets the net present worth equal to zero is the true average annual rate of return. In the above example the rate of return would be 10 per cent. One can check this answer by computing the future worth of an investment compounded at 10 per cent for two years.

$$\text{Future worth} = 10.0 \ (1 + .10)^2$$
$$\text{Future worth} = 12.1 \ \text{thousand}$$

Notice that in the above example, the investment is entered as a negative amount and the return as a positive amount. It is important to realize that, from the perspective of the model and the respective computer program, in any year an investment is made or increased only if there is a negative net cash flow for that year. As is common with most real-estate models, all transactions for any year are assumed to take place on the same day, here, on the last day of the year.

The rate of return computed from the cash flow with no loans (Appendix Table 1) is a rate return on the total project cost. While this figure ought to be of some interest to financial institutions that lend money, community builders are borrowers; that is, most community builders will leverage their investments by borrowing money at an interest rate which is lower than the rate of return for the unfinanced project. The model therefore must be able to compute a rate of return on equity, a rate of return on the investor's own money. This means that the program must be able to handle loan data.

With the loans, as with the other inputs, one could program any degree of flexibility. In the computer program, one can have any number of loans in any year. Each loan can have a separate interest rate and a separate pay back schedule. Given the number of principle payments, principle-free years, if any, and a pay-out relationship triggered to land sales, the program actually computes the repayment schedule.

At the end of a particular series of loans, the program computes a new cash-flow table and a new rate of return based on the particular equity position indicated by the loan series (Appendix Table 2). Once a rate of return for a particular loan series is computed, the program computes the increment in sales prices which would be necessary to result in some predetermined rate of return.

The results of running a set of data under different sales assumptions and different loan assumptions are shown in Appendix Table 3. It takes less than ten seconds of IBM 7094 computer time to compute the rate of return for each set of assumptions. While it takes some effort to collect the input data, once this is collected, it takes little effort to key punch the data and run it through the computer. To write the program, however, took five months.

APPENDIX TABLE 1

Eutopia: Cash Movement with No Loans of Eutopia

Year	1	2	3	4	5
1. Total sales	0.0	0.0	0.0	2,550.0	4,610.0
2. Cash proceeds	0.0	0.0	0.0	1,275.0	3,580.0
3. Special cost	0.0	0.0	0.0	0.0	0.0
4. Project cost	19,227.0	0.0	660.0	−20.0	18,215.0
5. Unit cost	0.0	0.0	0.0	0.0	0.0
6. Cost of sale	0.0	0.0	0.0	25.5	46.1
7. Tax	192.3	192.3	260.1	277.9	291.3
8. Total cost	19,419.3	192.3	920.1	283.4	18,552.4
9. Net movement	−19,419.3	−192.3	−920.1	991.6	−14,972.4
10. Cumulative movement	−19,419.3	−19,611.6	−20,531.7	−19,540.0	−34,512.4

Year	11	12	13	14	15[b]
1. Total sales	11,890.0	11,890.0	11,890.0	7,590.0	9,951.0
2. Cash proceeds	10,020.0	11,890.0	11,890.0	9,740.0	13,746.0
3. Special cost	0.0	0.0	0.0	0.0	0.0
4. Project cost	2,164.8	2,164.8	2,164.8	2,164.8	2,164.8
5. Unit cost	0.0	0.0	0.0	0.0	0.0
6. Cost of sale	118.9	118.9	118.9	75.9	99.5
7. Tax	235.6	161.5	87.4	45.7	0.0
8. Total cost	2,519.3	2,445.2	2,371.1	2,286.4	2,264.3
9. Net movement	7,500.7	9,444.8	9,518.8	7,453.6	11,481.7
10. Cumulative movement	−14,257.9	−4,813.1	4,705.7	12,159.3	23,640.9

[a] At the end of year 10 there remains 6,441 units of land. Using the latest sales price, the gross worth of this land is $36,780. Since the average sales rate of the past 5 years is 990 units per year, it is assumed that this land will be sold in 6.5 years. The cost of selling this land is 20 per cent of sales price. Discounting this

APPENDIX TABLE 1 (Continued)
Eutopia: Cash Movement with No Loans of Eutopia

6	7	8	9	10a	1–10
8,150.0	8,150.0	8,150.0	8,150.0	8,150.0	47,910.0
6,380.0	8,150.0	8,150.0	8,150.0	8,150.0	43,835.0
0.0	250.0	0.0	0.0	0.0	250.0
0.0	0.0	–40.0	150.0	24,063.0	62,255.0
0.0	0.0	0.0	0.0	0.0	0.0
81.5	81.5	81.5	81.5	81.5	479.1
300.6	299.9	289.2	268.4	237.6	2,609.4
382.1	631.4	330.7	499.9	24,382.1	65,593.5
5,997.9	7,518.6	7,819.3	7,650.1	–16,232.1	–21,758.5
–28,514.5	–20,995.9	–13,176.6	–5,526.5	–21,758.5	–21,758.5

16	17	18	19	20	1–20
0.0	0.0	0.0	–0.0	–0.0	101,121.0
0.0	0.0	0.0	0.0	0.0	101,121.0
0.0	0.0	0.0	0.0	0.0	250.0
0.0	0.0	0.0	0.0	0.0	73,079.0
0.0	0.0	0.0	0.0	0.0	0.0
0.0	0.0	0.0	0.0	0.0	1,011.2
0.0	0.0	0.0	0.0	0.0	3,139.8
0.0	0.0	0.0	0.0	0.0	77,480.0
0.0	0.0	0.0	0.0	0.0	23,640.9
0.0	0.0	0.0	0.0	0.0	23,640.9

cost over the expected sales period, the value of the unsold land is computed to be $20,377. The rate of return at the end of year 10 is –0.8 per cent.

[b] At the end of year 15 there is no unsold land. The rate of return at the end of year 15 is 6.4 per cent.

APPENDIX TABLE 2

Eutopia: Cash Movement with Loans, Loan Series 2

Year	1	2	3	4	5
1. Total sales	0.0	0.0	0.0	2,550.0	4,610.0
2. Cash proceeds	0.0	0.0	0.0	1,275.0	3,580.0
3. New loans	14,564.5	144.2	690.1	212.5	13,914.3
4. Total cash in	14,564.5	144.2	690.1	1,487.5	17,494.3
5. Development exp.	19,419.3	192.3	920.1	283.4	18,552.4
6. Loan balance	0.0	13,524.1	12,616.9	12,198.1	11,282.4
7. Loan interest	0.0	873.0	820.1	798.4	744.6
8. Loan principle	0.0	1,040.3	1,051.3	1,108.9	1,128.2
9. Total debt serv.	0.0	1,914.2	1,871.5	1,907.3	1,872.9
10. Total cash out	19,419.3	2,106.5	2,791.7	2,190.7	20,425.2
11. Net movement	−4,854.8	−1,962.3	−2,101.5	−703.2	−2,931.0
12. Cumulative movement	−4,854.8	−6,817.1	−8,918.6	−9,621.8	−12,552.8

Year	11	12	13	14	15[b]
1. Total sales	11,890.0	11,890.0	11,890.0	7,590.0	9,951.0
2. Cash proceeds	10,020.0	11,890.0	11,890.0	9,740.0	13,746.0
3. New loans	1,889.5	1,833.9	1,778.4	1,714.8	0.0
4. Total cash in	11,909.5	13,723.9	13,668.4	11,454.8	13,746.0
5. Development exp.	2,519.3	2,445.2	2,371.1	2,286.4	2,264.3
6. Loan balance	25,010.1	19,985.7	14,294.4	7,734.0	0.0
7. Loan interest	1,887.1	1,614.0	1,309.2	964.4	566.9
8. Loan principle	6,441.5	6,813.9	7,525.2	8,338.8	9,448.8
9. Total debt serv.	8,328.6	8,527.9	8,834.4	9,303.2	10,015.7
10. Total cash out	10,848.0	10,873.1	11,205.5	11,589.6	12,280.1
11. Net movement	1,061.5	2,750.8	2,462.8	−134.8	1,465.9
12. Cumulative movement	1,333.7	4,084.5	6,547.3	6,412.6	7,878.5

[a] At the end of year 10 there remains 6,441 units of land. Using the latest sales price, the gross worth of this land is $36,780. Since the average sales rate of the past 5 years is 990 units per year, it is assumed that this land will be sold in 6.5 years. The cost of selling this land is 20 per cent of sales price. Discounting this

APPENDIX TABLE 2 (Continued)
Eutopia: Cash Movement with Loans, Loan Series 2

6	7	8	9	10a	1–10
8,150.0	8,150.0	8,150.0	8,150.0	8,150.0	47,910.0
6,380.0	8,150.0	8,150.0	8,150.0	8,150.0	43,835.0
286.6	473.6	248.0	374.9	18,286.5	49,195.2
6,666.6	8,623.6	8,398.0	8,524.9	26,436.5	93,030.2
382.1	631.4	330.7	499.9	24,382.1	65,593.5
22,601.4	20,260.9	18,048.1	15,574.4	13,165.1	13,165.1
1,511.8	1,373.3	1,244.1	1,097.8	957.0	9,420.9
2,595.3	2,627.1	2,686.3	2,721.7	2,784.2	17,743.5
4,107.1	4,000.4	3,930.4	3,819.5	3,741.2	27,164.4
4,489.2	4,631.8	4,261.0	4,319.4	28,123.2	92,758.0
2,177.4	3,991.8	4,137.0	4,205.5	−1,686.7	272.2
−10,375.4	−6,383.6	−2,246.6	1,958.9	272.2	272.2

16	17	18	19	20	1–20
0.0	0.0	0.0	−0.0	−0.0	101,121.0
0.0	0.0	0.0	0.0	0.0	101,121.0
0.0	0.0	0.0	0.0	0.0	56,411.8
0.0	0.0	0.0	0.0	0.0	157,532.8
0.0	0.0	0.0	0.0	0.0	77,480.0
0.0	0.0	0.0	0.0	0.0	0.0
0.0	0.0	0.0	0.0	0.0	15,762.4
0.0	0.0	0.0	0.0	0.0	56,411.8
0.0	0.0	0.0	0.0	0.0	72,174.2
0.0	0.0	0.0	0.0	0.0	149,654.3
0.0	0.0	0.0	0.0	0.0	7,878.5
7,878.5	7,878.5	7,878.5	7,878.5	7,878.5	7,878.5

cost over the expected sales period, the value of the unsold land is computed to be $20,377. The rate of return at the end of year 10 is 8.4 per cent.

b At the end of year 15 there is no unsold land. The rate of return at the end of year 15 is 7.6 per cent.

APPENDIX TABLE 3

Eutopia: Variations in Rate of Return as a Result of Varied Sales Prices and Financing

	No Financing	Financing: 75 Per Cent of Cost 6 Per Cent Interest	Financing: 75 Per Cent of Cost 4 Per Cent Interest
Sales price 10 per cent down	4.0	loss	4.0
Normal sales price	6.4	7.4	11.2
Sales price 10 per cent up	8.7	13.2	16.4

It is indeed strange to the cautious that any community builder, or at least anyone financing a community builder, should not have developed such a computer program. Sunset International Petroleum has done some preliminary work on a model and has completed a working simplified program. And an IBM 1401 program which does not compute a rate of return has been developed by Price-Waterhouse for Wilsey, Ham and Blair and has been used by a few community builders.[5] While it is true that a computer makes it easier to "play" with a plan in order to compare alternative development schemes, one could perform the same work by hand. Perhaps the willingness and the ability to act without such a program is what separates consultants from entrepreneurs.

[5] John B. Spring and L. B. Reehl "Forecasting Financial Results . . . Case Study of a Modern Technique," *The Price Waterhouse Review*, X, 1, (Spring 1965).

Wilsey, Ham and Blair: Development Design Department, *Factsville, U. S. A.* (October, 1964).

Sunset International Petroleum Corporation, "A Computer Program for the Profile Analysis of Land Development." (December, 1964).